29 [date]

Dear Paul

Thank you for all your support, leadership and fun along the way.

All the best for whatever you do next, if you're looking for inspiration turn to page 184.

Love Ping & Lucy.

HONG KONG FOOD & CULTURE

2nd Edition

Hong Kong Food & Culture: 2nd Edition
Author: ADELE WONG
Translator: CHAN SIN YAN
Editor: SEAN HEBERT (1ST EDITION)
Creative Directors: JENNA LI, EDMUND IP (1ST EDITION)
Proofreaders: EDWIN LIEM, DIANE DANG (1ST EDITION)
Photographer: ALAN PANG
Recipes Creator: BLACKIE HUI

Copyright © 2020 Man Mo Media Limited. All rights reserved.

No part of this publication may be reproduced, distributed, or transmitted in any form or by any means, including photocopying, recording, or other electronic or mechanical methods, without the prior written permission of the publisher, except in the case of brief quotations embodied in critical reviews and certain other non-commercial uses permitted by copyright law. For permission requests, write to the publisher at books@manmomedia.com.

2nd Edition: 2020
Printed in China, Published in Hong Kong

1st Edition: 2016

ISBN 978-988-77560-3-3

www.manmomedia.com

PING YUM PRONUNCIATION GUIDE

We have developed our own Cantonese pronunciation guide that doesn't follow Jyutping, Yale or any other official romanization system. Our goal is to spell out the Cantonese words in the simplest, most intuitive way possible via the English alphabet. It's not exactly foolproof or scientific, but we hope it'll make your Cantonese learning journey easier. We're unofficially calling it the Ping Yum (拼音 ping3 yum1) system.

CONSONANTS

B - **b**ut, **b**oy
P - **p**at, **p**ig
M - **m**om, **m**an
F - **f**an, **f**un

D - **d**og
T - **t**omorrow
N - **n**o, **n**anny
L - **l**uck, **l**ot

G - **g**o
K - **c**at
H - **h**ow

Gw - **gw**en
Kw - **qu**ick
W - **w**ait

J - close to **j**ay (between **dz** and **zh**)
Ch - **ch**urch

S - **s**and, **s**o
Y - **y**ou, **y**awn

NASAL SOUNDS

Mm - hm**mm**

VOWELS / FINALS

Ah - p**a**pa
Ahm - **ar**m (British pronunciation)
Ahn - C**an**nes
Ahng - **An**gkor
Ahp - c**ap**
Aht - **at** with silent t
Ahk - bl**ack** with silent k
Ai - b**i**te, b**i**ke
Ao - c**ow**
Au - **ou**ch, **out**
Aw - s**aw**
Awn - l**awn**, d**awn**
Awng - H**ong** K**ong**
Awk - h**awk** with silent k
Awt - h**ot** with silent t
Ay - h**ay**

Eck - b**eck** with silent k
Ee - k**ey**
Eem - s**eem**, t**eam**
Een - s**een**
Eep - p**eep** with silent p

Eet - n**eat** with silent t
Eh - **e**ver
Em - **Em**ulate
Eng - s**ang**
Ep - l**ep**rosy with silent p

Ick - s**ick** with silent k
Ing - s**ing**
Iu - p**ew**

O / Oh - s**o**, t**oe**
Ohng - d**on't** with silent g ending
Oo - b**oo**, w**oo**
Oon - sp**oon**
Ook - c**ook** with silent k
Oot - b**oot** with silent t
Ooi - ph**ooey** (said quickly)
Oy - t**oy**, s**oy**
Urng - Ch**urch** with silent g ending

U - close to l**ew**d
Uck - y**uck** with silent k
Uht - close to p**ut**
Un - s**un**
Ui - fengsh**ui** (or **oei**l in French)
Une - close to imm**une**
Urk - l**urk** with silent k
Ute - close to m**ute** with silent t
Uhn - d**uh**, with an n ending
Um - s**um**, l**um**
Un - s**un**, r**un**
Ung - s**ung**
Up - p**up** with silent p
Ur - f**ur**
Utt - b**ut** with a silent t

Ye - b**ye**, r**ye**

Cantonese is a very tonal language. In fact, every word in Cantonese can be attributed to a note/note blend on the western classical major scale.

TONE (same as Jyutping)	1	2	3	4	5	6
	mi	do-re	do	so	ti-do	ti

Although I was born in Hong Kong, my family emigrated to Toronto in the early 90s. I was still a child then, and effectively spent my formative years in a completely different environment than that of my native city.

Children absorb culture and languages like sponges. My English soon became better than my Cantonese, and my favorite foods changed from deep-fried fish balls from a hawker cart in Rennie's Mill village (present-day Tiu Keng Leng), to baked potatoes with butter and chives.

To make sure we didn't completely lose our roots, my parents sent my sister and I to Chinese classes every Friday night, and made fried rice for our school lunches. But over time, my Cantonese just got worse, and I began to appreciate a slice of pizza more than a bowl of double-boiled pork bone soup.

When I relocated back to Hong Kong for a work opportunity, I experienced a huge dose of reverse culture shock. The city where I was born had become something foreign. The towering skyscrapers, the bustling alleyways, the crowded tables at the dai pai dong stalls all felt overwhelming.

Fast forward to today. These pages in front of you are my attempt at rediscovering a heritage that I hadn't really lost, but at the same time never had a chance to fully grasp while growing up abroad. And what better way to learn about Hong Kong, than through its rich culinary offerings?

The story of Hong Kong can be found in humble cha chaan teng restaurants, old-school dim sum houses, colorful wet markets, classic herbal tea shops. It's told by local butchers, street food hawkers, third-generation noodle-makers continuing their grandparents' legacy.

Hong Kong's Cantonese connection and its colonial past can be glimpsed from a simple bowl of macaroni noodle soup. Hongkongers' holistic approach to health is embodied in a glass of cooling five-flower tea. The city's coastal advantage can be easily gleaned via its citizens' love of seafood, both dried and fresh. And on and on and on.

This second edition of the book is essentially the same as the first, but with minor corrections and updates. Some establishments we had interviewed have since sadly closed — but their stories remain as powerful and poignant as ever.

Adele Wong
Author

OVERVIEW 8

CLASSIC DISHES AND ESSENTIAL INGREDIENTS 14

SAUCES, OILS, PASTES AND CONDIMENTS 34

RICE, NOODLES, DUMPLINGS 64

LOCAL RESTAURANTS 100

WET MARKET CULTURE 140

STREET FOOD CULTURE 164

DIM SUM AND TEA CULTURE 188

TRADITIONAL CHINESE MEDICINE 212

HERBS, SPICES, PRESERVED GOODS 232

FOOD FOR EVERY OCCASION 266

DINING ETIQUETTE 288

COOKING TECHNIQUES 298

TABLEWARE, UTENSILS AND COOKING EQUIPMENT 316

REFERENCES 336

OVERVIEW OF HONG KONG CUISINE

SCIANSI
Thienin
Zinan
Pinian
Lugan
Fun
Xantung
Carcen
XENSI
Sigan fu
Chiamcheu
Chaifun
XANTVNG
La Sior
Coree
Corei
Honan
Caramoran R.
Golfe de Nanquim
Ancium
HONAN
Paunin
Caisuim
Xanuchi
I. Quelpaerts
Cacian
NANQVIN
Nanquim
Cinthu
HVQVAM
Scianhay
Cipan
Wchang
IAPON
Nan ciam
Viceu
Hiamheu
QVICHEV
Sinan
KIAMSI
CHEQVIAM
Quicheo
Iuenceu
Lequeo
Chingtu
I. Siku
C. Liampo
Liampo
Nangam
Fucheu
SVSCVEM
I. Cheuxan
les Roys mages
FVQVIEM
Muilin
Nanhum
I. Formose ou Pakan
Chaokin
Chincheo
Zelande
QVANSI
Quanci
Queilin
VNAM
Canton
TON
Vanka
Tayouan
CAN
Xauqui
Amacao
Yunnam
MER DE LA CHINE
I. Sanchoan
Kincenfu
I. Aynaon
CHINE
150
160
170
30
20

Hong Kong (香港 *hurng1 gawng2*) ("fragrant harbor") is a collection of beautiful islands and mountainous terrains in southeast China. The city once belonged to Guangdong province (廣東省 *gwawng2 dohng1 sahng2*), a coastal landmass that faces the South China Sea and borders Fujian, Jiangxi, Hunan and Guangxi to the north, east and west. Currently, Hong Kong is an autonomously governed region with its own set of laws. To really understand its unique position in the Greater China narrative, it is necessary to take a step back and look at the city's historical and geographical influences.

Hong Kong started out as a humble fishing village blessed with a few rice paddies — a big contrast to the skyscrapers and concrete jungle that we see today.

To its north is Guangzhou (廣州 *gwawng2 jau1*) (formerly Canton), the capital city of Guangdong. Guangzhou was a trading port for foreign merchants in the late-17th to the mid-19th century, and at one point, it was the only official port of entry for European traders, under a setup known as the Canton System (一口通商 *yutt1 hau2 tohng1 surng1*).

A significant portion of the population in Guangdong province speaks a Chinese language known as Cantonese (廣東話 *gwawng2 dohng1 wah2*), in contrast to China's official language of Putonghua (普通話 *po2 tohng1 wah2*) ("common tongue"). In fact, many Chinese food terms that have been translated into English originate from Cantonese. Words like wok (鑊 *wawk6*), wonton (雲吞 *wun4 tun1*) and dim sum (點心 *deem2 sum1*) are just a few examples.

Cantonese cuisine (粵菜 *yute6 choy3*) refers to the cuisine that comes out of Guangdong province, and is considered one of eight major Chinese culinary styles — alongside the cuisines of Sichuan, Anhui, Zhejiang, Shandong, Hunan, Fujian and Jiangsu. In short: China is a country with a rich and diverse culinary history that dates back thousands of years, and Cantonese cuisine is one prominent piece of the whole.

Cantonese cuisine in general is known for its seafood-based dishes (both fresh and dried), its reliance on sauces, its roast meats, and its dim sum. Broadly speaking, Cantonese cuisine also emcompasses a few distinct regional styles — like the intense flavors of Chaozhou (潮州 *chiu4 jau1*) city, and the simple homey dishes of the Hakka people (客家 *hahk3 gah1*) who inhabited different parts of China, including Guangdong. While Cantonese cuisine is the undisputed backbone of Hong Kong cuisine, and the two terms are often used interchangeably due to Hong Kong's prominence on the world stage, it is more accurate to say that Hong Kong cuisine is a unique variation of Cantonese cuisine.

Now, onto a very different side of Hong Kong history. The area that we currently refer to as Hong Kong had been under Chinese jurisdiction for thousands of years. But the city as we know it today, really began when it came under British colonial rule in the 19th century.

Hong Kong Island officially became a British Crown Colony in 1842, following the conclusion of the First Opium War. The war resulted from trade disagreements between the British and Chinese governments — the British essentially pushed for opium to be legally exported to China to balance out the former's demand for Chinese goods. The Chinese resisted, and this led to destructive naval warfare in the waters around Guangdong. The British later managed to secure the Kowloon peninsula, the New Territories as well as the outlying islands of Hong Kong after a second similarly themed war coupled with impressively aggressive negotiations. The city underwent a brief period of Japanese occupation during World War II, but the British resumed their reign after the war.

Although the different parts of modern-day Hong Kong were leased or ceded to the British during different years and under different circumstances, the entire territory was handed back to the Chinese government in 1997, where it has since remained under Chinese rule. However, a joint declaration signed by both governments allows Hong Kong to be governed as a Special Administrative Region (SAR) until 2047, under an official "One Country, Two Systems" approach that gives the city a high degree of autonomy.

China has experienced different waves of dramatic emigration throughout its modern history, and for various reasons beyond the scope of this book, a significant portion of these emigrants were of Cantonese origin. In the 19th century, Guangdong men were shipped to the Americas for railroad work (North America) or forced manual labor (Peru, Cuba). The period just before the 1997 Handover to China saw a large exodus of Hongkongers to western countries like the United Kingdom, Canada, the United States and Australia, due to political uncertainty at home. Even though Hongkongers and Cantonese speakers make up only a tiny fraction of the overall Chinese population, oftentimes they have become the de facto Chinese representatives — and by extension, Chinese food ambassadors — in the nations to which they relocated.

It is no coincidence that a disproportionate number of Chinese restaurants outside of China have historically been Cantonese-style restaurants — although that landscape has started to change in recent years, as emigrants from different parts of China choose to settle overseas.

In the meantime, Hong Kong is home to people of many different backgrounds. The majority of the population is ethnically Han Chinese, but this seemingly homogenous pool can be further divided into indigenous villagers (defined as native inhabitants who settled in Hong Kong's New Territories before British rule); and the more recent migrants from various parts of Guangdong, Shanghai and the rest of China — many of whom had to flee their hometowns during the civil and international wars that rocked the country.

With its colonial past and Commonwealth connections; its current — and some might argue, eroding — status as an international financial center and a commercial gateway to mainland China; its low tax rates; and its obsession with hiring domestic and manual laborers from abroad; Hong Kong nowadays is home to many nationals from countries like the United Kingdom, Canada, Australia, the United States, India, the Philippines, Indonesia and many, many more.

With this interesting set of circumstances as backdrop, one can now hopefully begin to appreciate the fascinating origins of Hong Kong cuisine. It is as much about traditional Cantonese techniques as it is about east-meets-west fusion. It is built on sound culinary fundamentals, and yet it is as innovative and adaptive as it gets. Hong Kong cuisine is truly in a class of its own.

CLASSIC DISHES
AND ESSENTIAL INGREDIENTS

ong Kong cuisine is very diverse, and it can get tricky trying to pinpoint exactly all the elements that make it what it is. But it's well worth it to take a glimpse at a few classic dishes that Hongkongers make at home, as well as some of the more common raw ingredients that can be found in a home kitchen, to gain an understanding of what sets Hong Kong cooking apart from the rest.

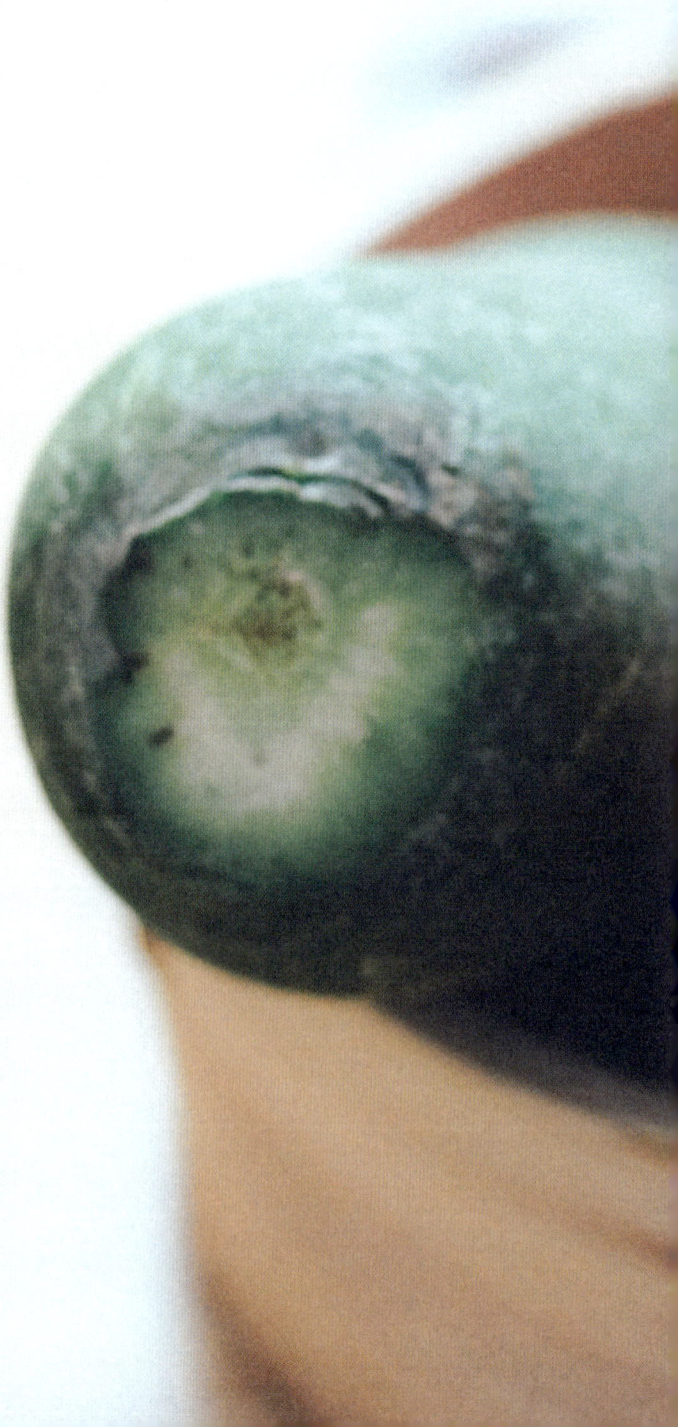

ESSENTIAL INGREDIENTS

❶ GINGER
薑 *gurng1*

Ginger is a favorite for Hong Kong cooks. The fresh spice is typically sliced up and wok-fried with other ingredients under high heat, to add a fragrant kick to dishes. Read more about ginger's function in Cantonese cuisine in the Herbs and Spices chapter.

❷ GARLIC
蒜頭 *sune3 tau4*

Garlic might not be specifically associated with Cantonese cuisine, but it's a ubiquitous ingredient that pairs particularly well with the wok. The garlic is commonly diced into tiny pieces and used in stir-fried dishes.

Diced garlic and sliced up ginger are oftentimes combined and tossed into a sizzling, oiled wok in a process called "bao hurng" (爆香 *bao3 hurng1*) (literally, to make fragrant through toss-frying). When done right, you can hear the satisfying crackle of the wok as the garlic pieces turn golden brown.

❸ CILANTRO
芫荽 *yune4 sai1*

Cilantro (also known as Chinese parsley or coriander) is a very popular ingredient for Chinese soups, and its pungent aroma is used to enhance the flavors of dishes.

❹ SCALLION
蔥 *chohng1*

Scallion — also sometimes called spring onion (大蔥 *dye6 chohng1*) in English, although the two are slightly different specimens — is a wonderfully versatile plant that can be used as a garnish in many Cantonese dishes. Sometimes the chopped-up scallion pieces are tossed into the wok along with the other ingredients, but oftentimes they are sprinkled on top of noodle broths and already cooked dishes to add flavor and color.

Different types of scallion are available during different seasons of the year. In winter, red scallion (紅頭蔥 *hohng4 tau4 chohng1*) with purplish bulbs are sold in abundance, while in spring and summer the more common white-bulbed scallion (白頭蔥 *bahk6 tau4 chohng1*) takes over market stall shelves.

CHICKEN
雞 *gai1*

Chicken is a must for Hongkongers, and the bird can be consumed from head to toe. Steamed chicken feet make a popular dim sum dish, and whole chicken is sometimes served along with its decapitated head at restaurants and roast meat shops. At home, fried chicken wings make for an easy dish while stir-fried and steamed chicken meat are also common concoctions. Although a rarer sight these days, there are still a few live chicken stalls in wet markets across the city that offer to butcher and de-pluck the animal upon purchase.

Lots of wet market stalls stock chilled-fresh chicken (冰鮮雞 *bing1 seen1 gai1*): birds that have been butchered at a farm on the day of purchase, then chilled to just above zero degree Celsius. When you buy chicken from a wet market stall, you can bring the bird back whole, in halves, or chopped up to your liking. Generally speaking, the chicken always comes with skin and bones attached.

PORK
猪肉 *ju1 yook6*

Pork, especially in minced form, is Hongkongers' go-to red meat. MInced pork can be steamed on its own, stuffed into dumplings, or turned into pork balls. It's easy to handle and makes for a failsafe home-cooked dish. Pork chops also feature in home dishes, typically pan-fried and seasoned with soy sauce or ketchup and sliced onion. Pork bone-based soups and broths are another easy favorite, sometimes paired with corn, carrots, pork meat, fish meat and apricot kernels. You'll notice that most butcheries in Hong Kong are dedicated to the pig, and beef-based stalls are more of a rare sight.

FISH
魚 *yu2*

Home cooks love to work with fresh fish procured from the wet market. Both freshwater and saltwater fish from all over the world are quite popular with Hongkongers. Large fish like grouper (石斑 *seck6 bahn1*) and grass carp (鯇魚 *wahn5 yu2*) are usually sold chopped up in pieces, while smaller fish like yellowfin sea bream (黃腳鱲 *wawng4 gurk3 lahp6*) (pictured) can be bought whole at wet market stalls. Once you pick your fish at a wet market stall, it gets de-scaled and gutted for easy preparation at home. Steamed or pan-fried, fish are usually treated whole. They are de-scaled on purchase, but the skin and bones remain intact.

PRAWNS / SHRIMP
蝦 *hah1*

To Hongkongers, prawns pair very well with pork — and you'll frequently find the two types of meat minced together and used as filling for dumplings. De-shelled prawns can be stir-fried with scrambled eggs, noodles and vegetables. Prawns with head and shell intact, sometimes still swimming, can be found at wet market stalls and are steamed, stir-fried or deep-fried as a dish on their own. No wonder why this versatile crustacean is especially popular in the home kitchen.

LEAFY GREENS
菜 *choy3*

Leafy greens is a vague term, but to be honest, it pretty much summarizes the entire vegetable category for Hongkongers. Any plant that comes with a stalk and plenty of leaves can be steamed, scalded or stir-fried and stand as a dish on its own. We talk more about the different types of leafy greens in the Wet Market chapter.

TOFU
豆腐 *dau6 foo6*

Tofu, or bean curd, is a pretty generic term. This fermented soybean product can be bought fresh from the wet markets or packaged from shop shelves, and comes in all shapes, textures and sizes. Some are velvety smooth (perfect for steaming), some come with tough yellow skins (good for high-heat treatment in a wok), while some are dry and rough (and an excellent stir-fry companion to meat and veggies).

CANTONESE LYE WATER
鹼水 *gahn2 sui2*

Cantonese lye water's (also known as potassium carbonate solution) role in Cantonese cuisine is quite unique and definitely deserves a mention. Besides being used industrially to make noodles more springy in texture, Cantonese lye water can also be used to give ingredients like glutinous rice a golden hue. Adding a few drops of lye water to the water used to boil your leafy greens can also give the vegetables a vivid green shade.

CONGEE
WITH CENTURY EGGS AND PORK

皮蛋排骨粥 *pay4 dahn2 pye4 gwutt1 jook1* • 75 min • 1 night • 4-5 persons

Congee is the type of comfort food that Hongkongers crave when they are feeling a bit under the weather — it's the equivalent of western-style chicken soup, if you will. Congee is also a popular breakfast item.

INGREDIENTS

1 cup rice kernels 米 *mai5*
1/2 catty (600g) spare ribs 排骨 *pye4 gwutt1*
2 century eggs 皮蛋 *pay4 dahn2*
Peanut oil 花生油 *fah1 sung1 yau4*
Peanuts 花生 *fah1 sung1*
Dried tangerine peel 陳皮 *chun4 pay4*
Salt 鹽 *yeem4*

METHOD

1. Rinse spare ribs with water and marinate with lots of salt, overnight.

2. Soak rice kernels in water (with a drop of oil added in) for 15 minutes before cooking. Fill pot with 10 cups of water and boil over high heat. When water is boiling, add rice kernels and dried tangerine peel to pot. Boil for around 1 hour, until rice combines with water. Place a pair of chopsticks on top of the pot to break the froth that forms.

3. Meanwhile, cut century eggs into four pieces. Squeeze spare ribs with your hands at least a dozen times to get a more intense flavor from the meat.

4. When the rice combines with water, add spare ribs and century eggs into mixture. Cook for 15 minutes more and serve.

STEAMED CHICKEN WITH PRESERVED PORK SAUSAGE, DRIED DAYLILY PETALS, DRIED DONKO SHIITAKE, AND CLOUD EAR

臘腸金針冬菇雲耳蒸雞

lahp6 churng2 gum1 jum1 dohng1 goo1 wun4 yee5 jing1 gai1

⏱ 15-20 min   🍴 1 night   🍽 4 persons

Steaming is an essential technique in Cantonese kitchens, and it's also one of the healthiest, quickest ways to cook a meal. While steamed fish and dumplings are relatively mainstream Chinese dishes, steamed chicken is a lesser-known Cantonese classic.

INGREDIENTS

Half a chicken (skin, bones intact) 雞 *gai1*
1 preserved pork sausage 臘腸 *lahp6 churng2*
20 dried daylily petals 金針 *gum1 jum1*
6 dried donko shiitake 乾冬菇 *gawn1 dohng1 goo1*
1 handful cloud ear fungi 雲耳 *wun4 yee5*
Scallion 蔥 *chohng1*

Light soy sauce 豉油 *see6 yau4*
Peanut oil 花生油 *fah1 sung1 yau4*
Granulated sugar 砂糖 *sah1 tawng4*
Cornstarch 生粉 *sahng1 fun2*
Chinese rice wine 米酒 *mai5 jau2*

METHOD

1. The night before, cut chicken into small pieces (or have wet market butcher do it) and marinate with soy sauce, peanut oil, sugar, cornstarch and Chinese wine. Soak donko shiitake in water for at least 4 hours before cooking. Soak dried daylily petals and cloud ear in water at least 2 hours beforehand.

2. Slice preserved sausages and shiitake into pieces. Remove the black tip of the dried daylily. Mix chicken, dried lily flowers, shiitake, cloud ear and preserved sausages together and put on a plate.

3. Place steaming rack and add water into wok. Cook over high heat until water boils. Place ingredients into wok and steam for 15 to 20 minutes. Sprinkle chopped scallion on top for final garnish.

STEAMED EGG WITH FLOWER CRAB

花蟹肉碎蒸蛋 *fah1 hye5 yook6 sui3 jing1 dahn2*   🕐 10-15 min   🥄 10 min   👥 4-5 persons

Steamed egg is one of the simplest, tastiest dishes to make at home. In Cantonese culture, eggs appear regularly as a dinner item — and what better way to prepare them than with a quick beat and steam? This recipe is slightly more sophisticated than the typical household dish, working in a prized flower crab as centerpiece. Just remove the crab for the original recipe.

INGREDIENTS

3 chicken eggs 雞蛋 *gai1 dahn2*
1 flower crab 花蟹 *fah1 hye5*
100g minced pork 肉碎 *yook6 sui3*

Peanut oil 花生油 *fah1 sung1 yau4*
Granulated sugar 砂糖 *sah1 tawng4*
Salt 鹽 *yeem4*

METHOD

1. Rinse flower crab and remove internal organs. Marinate minced pork with peanut oil, sugar, and salt for at least 10 minutes.

2. Crack eggs into bowl. Add about 200mL of water (or at a ratio of 6 cracked eggshell halves of water for every egg). Add a little oil and salt. Beat eggs until bubbles begin to form.

3. Place minced pork and flower crab onto plate and add in egg mixture. Wrap plate in plastic wrap, and poke several holes at top of wrap. Place steaming rack into wok and add water. Heat over high heat until water boils.

4. Put plate into wok and steam for 10 to 15 minutes.

STEAMED POMFRET WITH SWEET AND SOUR PLUM

酸梅蒸鯧魚
sune1 mooi4 jing1 chawng1 yu2

🕐 15-20 min   ⏲ 30 min   👥 4 persons

Steamed fish is the true test of any aspiring Cantonese chef. Feel free to use different types of fish with this recipe, but do remember that cooking times might differ as a result.

INGREDIENTS

1 medium-sized pomfret 鯧魚 *chawng1 yu2*
1 sweet and sour plum 酸梅 *sune1 mooi4*
Fermented black soybeans 豆豉 *dau6 see6*
Salted soybean paste 麵豉 *meen6 see2*
Scallion 蔥 *chohng1*
Ginger 薑 *gurng1*

Garlic 蒜頭 *sune3 tau4*
Fish-steaming soy sauce 蒸魚豉油 *jing1 yu2 see6 yau4*
Granulated sugar 砂糖 *sah1 tawng4*
Peanut oil 花生油 *fah1 sung1 yau4*
Cornstarch 生粉 *sahng1 fun2*

METHOD

1. Rinse pomfret with salt water to mimic seawater environment, and to keep true flavor of fish. Chop up scallion and place into ice water to make pieces extra crunchy. Keep some scallion on the side for later use.

2. Soak fermented black soybeans in water for 30 minutes. Add sweet and sour plum as well as salted soybean paste and mash everything together.

3. Place scallion pieces on plate and place fish on top. Smear cornstarch onto fish skin. Spread paste onto top side of fish. Steam for about 10 minutes, turn off stove, and keep lid on for another 5 minutes to thoroughly cook fish.

4. While steaming, cut garlic and ginger into small pieces. When fish is almost ready, heat wok on medium heat. Stir-fry garlic and ginger with peanut oil, and pour on top of steamed fish for extra flavor. Add soy sauce, sugar and scallion to your preference, and serve.

STEAMED PORK PATTY WITH PRESERVED VEGETABLES

梅菜蒸肉餅
mooi4 choy3 jing1 yook6 beng2

🕐 15 min 🥄 20 min 👥 4 persons

Hongkongers love to steam things, and they love to eat pork. So this steamed pork patty recipe is a no-brainer. The hardest part is getting the pork to be the right texture. This will require a bit of manual labor — but you can take a shortcut and replace the pork belly with store-bought minced pork instead.

INGREDIENTS

1/2 catty (300g) pork belly
豬腩肉 *ju1 nahm5 yook6*

Preserved mustard greens
梅菜 *mooi4 choy3*

Scallion 蔥 *chohng1*

Soy sauce 豉油 *see6 yau4*

Granulated sugar 砂糖 *sah1 tawng4*

Salt 鹽 *yeem4*

Huadiao 花雕 *fah1 diu1*

Cornstarch 生粉 *sahng1 fun2*

METHOD

1. Rinse pork belly with water and cut into small fingertip-sized pieces. Press pork together and dice gently for about 1 minute, until meat slightly sticks together. Marinate minced pork with a bit of soy sauce, salt, cornstarch, sugar and huadiao for 10 to 15 minutes.

2. Rinse preserved mustard greens and place in bowl of water for about 10 minutes. Cut into fingertip-sized pieces.

3. Mix minced pork with preserved mustard greens, and place on plate. Steam for about 15 minutes or until the meat turns light brown. Chop up scallion, and sprinkle on pork patty when ready.

SAUCES, OILS, PASTES AND CONDIMENTS

ong Kong-style cooking involves a lot of sauces, pastes, flavored oils, and enhanced seasonings. Check out any local supermarket and you'll see jars, bottles and boxes of ready-made condiments vying for your attention. Whether they're used for cooking, dipping, marinating, coating or drizzling, condiments of all sorts of viscosities, flavors and colors comprise a major part of many Cantonese dishes.

Trying to decipher all the varieties and combinations available can be a dizzying task, but there are certainly some essential products that every Cantonese cook should stock in their kitchen or at least have a basic knowledge of.

SOY-BASED CONDIMENTS

Light Soy Sauce   Dark Soy Sauce

SOY SAUCE
豉油 *see6 yau4*

Soy sauce, which originated in China, is used in kitchens all across Asia. Cantonese-style soy sauce is usually made from fermented soybeans, wheat flour, water and salt — it is an essential seasoning that's used as commonly as salt, and gives foods an unparalleled umami flavor. In Hong Kong in particular, two types of soy sauce reign supreme. There's the ubiquitous light soy sauce (生抽 *sahng1 chau1*), a dark-brown-colored, runny, and intensely savory variety that is used for all types of cooking as well as to flavor and marinate foods. Light soy sauce is also frequently used as a condiment or dipping sauce for dishes.

Then there's the dark soy sauce (老抽 *lo5 chau1*), an aged light soy sauce with molasses or sweeteners and sometimes coloring added during fermentation. It is a darker-colored, slightly more viscous, but milder-tasting variety that's used to enhance the color of foods and to give them a delicate splash of flavor during cooking. Dark soy sauce is usually used in conjunction with light soy sauce rather than on its own, due to its gentler profile.

Besides dark and light soy sauce, there are also numerous variations and specializations of the condiment available. There's the esteemed "first draw" soy sauce (頭抽 *tau4 chau1*), which refers to the first, most concentrated extraction of a fermented soybean batch. There's "fish" soy sauce (蒸魚豉油 *jing1 yu2 see6 yau4*), a sweet and oily version made especially to pair with steamed fish. The list goes on.

Fermented Black Soybeans

Fermented Bean Sauce

Hoisin Sauce

FERMENTED BLACK SOYBEANS
豆豉 *dau6 see6*

Fermented black soybeans are a staple condiment in Cantonese cooking. Fresh soybeans — usually black-hulled ones, but not always — are first cooked, then drained and submerged in a saltwater solution for several months before being dried out in sunlight and sold as dusty, pungent black specks. The most common way of using fermented black soybeans is by first soaking a handful of them in water to rinse off their brine-covered exteriors, then dropping them on top of foods that are destined for the steamer or the wok. The beans give dishes a strong and distinctly fragrant savory profile. Salted black soybeans are also the natural inspiration behind many spin-off black-bean-based sauces.

FERMENTED BEAN SAUCE
豆瓣醬 *dau6 bahn2 jurng3*

Fermented bean sauce, or Doubanjiang, is actually a Sichuan-originated condiment typically made from chilies, fermented soybeans and broad beans, and a whole range of seasonings. The Cantonese version of fermented bean sauce would be lighter on the chilies, playing up the savory flavors instead. Fermented bean sauce is sometimes used in lieu of chili sauce as a dip for dumplings and meats. It can be used in stir-fries to give foods a sharp, salty kick.

HOISIN SAUCE
海鮮醬 *hoy2 seen1 jurng3*

The term hoisin means "seafood" in Cantonese, but don't be deceived: no marine-based creatures have gone into its making. Instead, hoisin sauce is a sweet, thick condiment made typically from ground Chinese spices and ground soybeans. Different brands would include different ingredients in their recipes, but the result is the same: a sauce that pairs particularly well with seafood.

Salted Soybean Paste

Fermented Bean Curd

Chu Hou Sauce

SALTED SOYBEAN PASTE
麵豉 *meen6 see2*

Salted soybean paste is a product derived from fermented yellow soybeans (the default soybean) — think of it as a Chinese variation of miso paste and a slightly more mellow version of fermented black soybeans. The "paste" actually consists of chunks of soybeans drowning in a savory liquid solution. Just like all the other soy-based products, salted soybean paste is used to enhance the flavors of a dish and give it a savory oomph. It's not to be confused with the red-hued fermented yellow soybean paste (黃醬 *wawng4 jurng3*) that's used in Beijing-style cuisine.

FERMENTED BEAN CURD
腐乳 *foo6 yu5*

Fermented bean curd is like the Chinese version of cheese: made from preserved tofu chunks (which in turn are made from soybeans) and extra seasonings, the end product is lumps of white bean curd suspended in a milky solution. The bean curd cubes can be mashed up and mixed with other ingredients, and used as the base sauce in stir-fried vegetables. Sometimes the bean curd cubes can be used as topping for plain congee. There are different strains of fermented bean curd products, including a red yeast rice (南乳 *nahm4 yu5*) variety that is frequently used in Chinese-style braised dishes.

CHU HOU SAUCE
柱侯醬 *chu5 hau4 jurng3*

Chu hou sauce is another sweet sauce, commonly used to marinate meats like pork, and added to braised and stewed dishes. It's made from ground soybeans, sesame, garlic and other seasonings.

SEAFOOD-BASED CONDIMENTS

XO Sauce

XO SAUCE
XO醬 *XO jurng3*

In the grand scheme of things, XO sauce is actually a relatively recent culinary development. Sometime in the 80s, someone in Hong Kong thought it was a good idea to combine bits and pieces of dried seafood with garlic, chilies and oil — and the result was a savory-spicy, semi-dry concoction that goes exceptionally well with all sorts of Cantonese dishes.

XO sauce has become so popular these days that esteemed restaurants across the city all make their own versions, and many contemporary recipes call for it as a key ingredient. XO sauce is quite versatile: it can be used in stir-fries, to top stews, and also as a standalone sauce to complement any food items that you feel can benefit from the feisty seasoning.

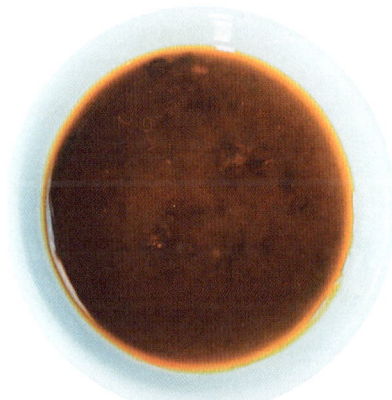
Sha Cha Sauce

SHA CHA SAUCE
沙茶醬 *sah1 chah4 jurng3*

Sha cha sauce originated from China's Chaoshan region and is a particularly popular dipping sauce for Hong Kong-style hot pot. It is made from shrimp, brill fish and a mix of Chinese spices, and has a sandy texture and slightly spicy flavor.

Liquid Shrimp Paste / Shrimp Sauce

SHRIMP PASTE
蝦膏 *hah1 go1*

Shrimp paste is a very common Southeast Asian condiment, and Hong Kong has its own version made from tiny silver shrimp that have been dried and fermented. Shrimp paste comes in blocks, is pale pink to gray in color, and is used sparingly to give dishes a fishy and savory character. Shrimp paste must be cooked to be consumed. There is also a variation of shrimp paste sold in liquidy sauce form called shrimp sauce (蝦醬 *hah1 jurng3*). Shrimp paste and shrimp sauce are both used in stir-fried vegetable dishes and specialty fried rice.

Oyster Sauce

OYSTER SAUCE
蠔油 *ho4 yau4*

Oyster sauce is a ubiquitous Hong Kong commodity, and its invention is credited to a man from Guangdong: Lee Kam-sheung, the father of Cantonese sauce empire Lee Kum Kee (李錦記 *lay5 gum2 gay5*). Oyster sauce is a thick, brown and sweet-savory paste that's traditionally made by slow-simmering oysters in water until the oysters' essence transfers to the liquid. The sauce can be used during cooking (Chinese-style braising is a popular method) and can also stand alone as a dipping sauce, usually for greens.

CHILI-BASED CONDIMENTS

Chili Sauce

Chili Oil

CHILI OIL
辣椒油 *laht6 jiu1 yau4*

The definition of chili oil is open to interpretation in Hong Kong. If you ask for it at a dim sum restaurant, you might end up getting a saucer of pure red chili oil, made from chili-infused vegetable oil. At local Chinese diners, fancier establishments and supermarkets, however, you might end up getting other kinds of chili oils, made in different styles and containing different ingredients. The chili oils might not be pure oils at all, and can contain chunks of chili bits, garlic, pepper, dried shrimp, sugar, soy sauce, salt, and other additions.

CHILI SAUCE
辣椒醬 *laht6 jiu1 jurng3*

Generally speaking, although chilies do appear in Hong Kong dishes from time to time, they are not a common ingredient. Chili sauce, on the other hand, is always featured on restaurant tables as a condiment that can be put on everything, from dumplings to noodles.

Chili sauce is a rather vague term in Hong Kong. But the most common variety you'll see at Cantonese restaurants is the homogenously orange-red sriracha-style sauce, which traces its origins to Thailand but is now used as a common condiment for dumplings and meats. Chinese chili sauce is typically made from a combination of chilies, garlic, vinegar, sugar and salt. Yu Kwen Yick is a well-known Hong Kong brand that specializes in this type of chili sauce.

OILS AND FATS

VEGETABLE OIL
植物油 *jick6 mutt6 yau4*

Hongkongers use all types of vegetable oils in their cooking. Peanut oil (花生油 *fah1 sung1 yau4*) is a particularly popular option for the home kitchen. Canola oil (芥花油 *gye3 fah1 yau4*), corn oil (粟米油 *sook1 mai5 yau4*) and sunflower seed oil (葵花籽油 *kwai4 fah1 jee2 yau4*) are also used. Although olive oil (橄欖油 *gahm3 lahm2 yau4*) is gaining ground in supermarkets across the city, it is not traditionally used in Cantonese cooking. Soybean oil (大豆油 *dye6 dau2 yau4*) is also used, but more in commercial kitchens rather than at home.

LARD
豬油 *ju1 yau4*

Lard is out of favor these days due to its perceived reputation as a less healthy strain of fat compared to vegetable oils and butter. But once upon a time it was a common ingredient in Cantonese cooking, prized for its rich, full aroma. Today, some traditional local diners and bakeries still tout pastries that are baked with lard, or various dishes topped or cooked with lard. Despite its relative demise in the contemporary culinary landscape, there are a number of loyalists — from food critics to older generations — that will swear by lard over any other fat or oil.

SESAME OIL
麻油 *mah4 yau4*

Sesame oil is a popular commodity in Hong Kong kitchens, and its main function is to enhance a dish with its distinct, powerful fragrance. Sesame oil is used sparingly, drizzled on top of ingredients and mixed in with other condiments, because its strong aroma can easily overpower a dish. A similar analogy would be the careful use of truffle oil in western cuisine.

WINES

ROSE LIQUOR
玫瑰露 *mooi4 gwai1 lo6*

Rose liquor originated in mainland China and is used sparingly in Cantonese-style stews and braised dishes for added fragrance. Rose liquor is actually a type of baijiu (白酒 *bahk6 jau2*) ("white wine") made from the sorghum plant and enhanced with roses and sugar.

HUADIAO
花雕 *fah1 diu1*

Huadiao is a type of huangjiu (黃酒 *wawng4 jau2*) ("yellow wine"), made from a cereal such as rice or sorghum. It's reddish brown in color and has a distinct aged-plum type of smell. It's frequently added to stews and broths to enhance flavor, or used to marinate poultry.

RICE WINE
米酒 *mai5 jau2*

The Chinese equivalent of sake, rice wine is made from fermented glutinous rice. It's a fragrant additive that is sometimes used to lightly season congee, rice dishes and meats.

VINEGAR-BASED SAUCES

BLACK RICE VINEGAR
黑醋 *hahk1 cho3*

Black rice vinegar looks just like soy sauce, but has a completely different flavor profile: it tastes smoky, malty and tart. Made from black glutinous rice (and sometimes sorghum or millet), black rice vinegar is used to season meat dishes and stir-fries. It can also be used as a dipping sauce for dumplings.

WHITE RICE VINEGAR
白醋 *bahk6 cho3*

White rice vinegar is made from glutinous rice. The vinegar is typically a pale yellow hue, and is used in dishes like the classic sweet and sour pork. Don't be deceived by its color: white rice vinegar is incredibly sharp and tangy.

RED RICE VINEGAR
浙醋 *jeet3 cho3*

Red rice vinegar traditionally gets its intense shade from moldy red yeast rice (紅米麴 *hohng4 mai5 gook1*). It is sometimes used as a dip for steamed dumplings. It is also a classic condiment for shark's fin soup (魚翅 *yu4 chee3*), a traditional Cantonese delicacy that is getting less and less popular due to concerns about industry-wide shark-finning practices.

OTHER CONDIMENTS

CHICKEN POWDER AND MSG
雞粉，味精 *gai1 fun2, may6 jing1*

Chicken powder (or flavor-enhanced chicken stock) is used to give a savory, umami kick to any dish. Similarly, pure MSG (monosodium glutamate) in its white crystalline form is also a prevalent additive.

SESAME SAUCE
芝麻醬 *jee1 mah4 jurng3*

Sesame sauce is a thick, light brown condiment that pairs especially well with rice noodle rolls and chicken and vegetable dishes. It's got a nutty aroma and is similar to peanut butter in appearance.

YELLOW CURRY SAUCE
咖喱醬 *gah3 lay1 jurng3*

Yellow curry is especially common in Hong Kong, found in everything from streetside fish balls to meat stews. Jars of the curry paste or sauce are available at local supermarkets, although you can also make your own with curry powder, sha cha sauce and other seasonings.

WORCESTERSHIRE SAUCE
喼汁 *geep1 jup1*

Worcestershire sauce was introduced to Hong Kong by the British while it was under colonial rule, and is popular with dim sum dishes like spring rolls and steamed beef balls. Worcestershire sauce contains vinegar, molasses, anchovies and tamarind and is extremely tart in taste. It looks a lot like soy sauce, with watery thin viscosity and a dark brown color.

FATHER OF PEARLS

CK Chan inherited his Lau Fau Shan oyster sauce-making business from his family. "Yu Hing was founded by my father in 1960," Chan says. "Lau Fau Shan is famous for its oysters, so it is the prime location for making oyster sauce. The sands used to be fine and the water quality was superb. But things have changed now."

"In the past, we Chinese did not eat oysters raw," he explains. "It wasn't part of the culture. We are near the coast and have many oysters, so oysters are just an everyday, normal food item. In Chinese cuisine, oysters are cooked with ginger and scallion, deep-fried, or stewed."

The sauce-making process is surprisingly simple. "You don't need many ingredients to make oyster sauce," Chan says. "You basically extract oyster juice from the oysters by boiling them. The oysters contain salt, so you don't need to add much seasoning. You continue cooking and condensing the oyster soup to a thicker liquid. We call this the oyster essence (蠔汁 *ho4 jup1*), which is 100 percent oyster juice. It costs about HK$100 a bottle. But [most people] won't pay $100 for a bottle, so we process the juice to about at most 50% concentration, which is the most premium oyster sauce you can get in the market."

"In the past, we Chinese did not eat oysters raw."

CK Chan, owner of
Yu Hing (裕興 *yu6 hing1*)

SAVORY SHRIMP

Shrimp paste is a specialty in the sleepy fishing village of Tai O, and Yick Cheong Ho is one of the dozens of family-style businesses that manufacture the highly localized product. "Shrimp paste-making depends a lot on the weather," owner Chui Chin Kam Yi tells us. "We only sun-dry our shrimp paste when we've got beautiful sunshine. We wash the dried silver shrimp, select the good ones, grind them, add salt, and then immediately lay them out into thin layers under the sunshine."

"After several hours, we turn the shrimp and sun-dry the back side. We turn the shrimp several times a day. After at least two days, it's proper shrimp paste. But sun-drying for about five days to about a week makes the best shrimp paste."

"We only sun-dry our shrimp paste when we've got beautiful sunshine."

Chiu Chin Kam Yi, owner of Yick Cheong Ho Fish Seller
(益昌號 *yick1 churng1 ho6*)

THE JOYS OF SOY

Kowloon Soy (or Mee Chun, to consumers outside of Hong Kong) is a widely respected homegrown soy sauce and soy-based sauce manufacturer. The company's factory in Yuen Long still dries its fermented soybean culture the traditional way: by loading everything into massive clay vats and letting the sun do its job. Kowloon Soy's current proprietor, Ken Wong, who is part of the original family that founded the brand, says that soy sauce made this way tastes and smells superior to the soy sauce produced by the quicker chemical hydrolysis process that some contemporary makers resort to.

Besides soy sauce, Kowloon Soy also makes many other types of soy-based products, pickled vegetables and Cantonese sauces to cover its bases. "Soy sauce takes three to four months to make, and we can't mass produce it," Wong explains. "A lot of the time, we cannot produce enough to match demand. And when it's raining, our numbers are affected."

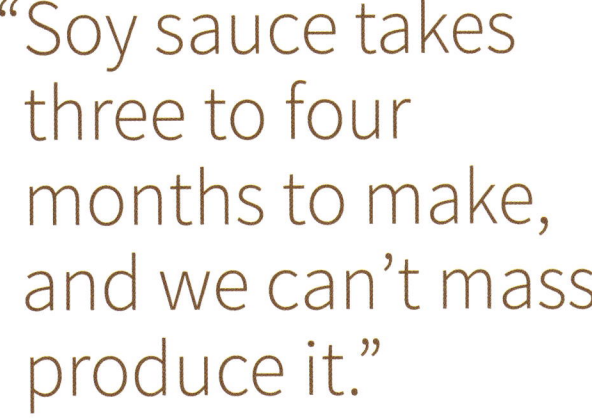

"Soy sauce takes three to four months to make, and we can't mass produce it."

Ken Wong, owner of Kowloon Soy (九龍醬園 *gau2 lohng4 jurng3 yune4*)

By contrast, products like chu hou sauce and salted soybean paste have higher turnover compared to soy sauce. But essentially, all of the soy-based sauces start out from the same batch of fermented soybeans: it's a matter of adding various ingredients like water, sugar and salt to start the differentiation process.

Although Kowloon Soy is a locally respected brand, a significant portion of the customer base is from countries like the Netherlands and the United Kingdom. There are also surprise hits from customers abroad. "We also make a plum sauce for Cantonese roast duck," Wong says, "and I noticed that the product was very highly sought after in the Netherlands. I wondered why, investigated, and found out that the people there were using it as jam for their breads!"

FRIED CHICKEN WINGS WITH SHRIMP PASTE

蝦醬炸雞翼
hah1 jurng3 jah3 gai1 yick6

🕐 15 min   🎣 1 night   👥 4-5 persons

Fried chicken wings are an all-time favorite dish in Hong Kong homes. In this recipe, the shrimp paste adds a delicious layer to the already tasty wings.

INGREDIENTS

20 pieces chicken wings 雞翼 *gai1 yick6*
1 tsp shrimp paste 蝦醬 *hah1 jurng3*
1 clove garlic 蒜瓣 *sune3 fahn2*

Ginger 薑片 *gurng1 peen2*
Cornstarch 生粉 *sahng1 fun2*
Peanut oil 花生油 *fah1 sung1 yau4*

METHOD

1. Cut ginger into several slices and peel garlic clove. Mix with shrimp paste, peanut oil (enough to cover each chicken wing entirely) and marinate wings overnight.

2. Pour cornstarch onto plate, and cover chicken wings in cornstarch. Heat oil in a pan over medium heat. Add chicken wings to pan, and fry for about 15 minutes. Poke a chopstick into chicken wing. If there's no blood, your chicken wings are ready to serve.

RICE, NOODLES, DUMPLINGS

Rice and noodles form the backbone of every Cantonese meal. Everything goes with a bowl of steaming jasmine rice, and when one wants to spice things up, a plate of noodles is a rebellious alternative. Simply put: we Hongkongers love our carbs.

RICE

Rice is believed to have originated from China thousands of years ago. Although there are countless types of rice in the world, most rice found and eaten in Asia belong to the species Oryza Sativa — a fancy name that encompasses Asia-grown grains of different shapes, colors and sizes. Within that species, there are two major varietals: the generally long-grained Indica (秈稻 *sahn3 do6*) and the generally short-grained Japonica (粳稻 *gung2 do6*). We say generally, because there are always exceptions — like the long-grained basmati rice used in Indian cuisine that is actually considered a type of Japonica.

LONG-GRAIN RICE
秈米 *sahn3 mai5*

Hongkongers prefer white rice, and the kernel of choice for most Hong Kong households is the thin, long-grained Indica white jasmine rice (香米 **hurng1 mai5**), sometimes referred to as Thai hom mali rice. The most well-known jasmine rice is grown in Thailand, and is thought to be particularly fragrant. Steamed rice, fried rice and congee (a type of rice porridge) all call for jasmine rice as the key ingredient.

Thailand, Japan and Taiwan are popular rice-growing countries for Hongkongers' tastes. China-grown rice is also available in Hong Kong — the country is easily the world's largest rice producer and a major rice exporter.

SHORT-GRAIN RICE
珍珠米 *jun1 ju1 mai5*

The short-grained Japonica is another type of rice that dominates supermarket shelves across the city. Japonica rice is more stubby, round and short compared to Indica rice, and the varieties available in Hong Kong are typically imported from Japan or Taiwan. Japonica rice tastes creamier and richer compared to the more delicate jasmine rice, and tends to be stickier in texture.

GLUTINOUS RICE
糯米 *naw6 mai5*

Glutinous rice, or sticky rice, is not as common as the non-sticky variety, but on occasion you will come across it bundled up in lotus leaf (荷葉飯 *haw4 yeep6 fahn6*), wrapped into bamboo leaf packets (糯米雞 *naw6 mai5 gai1*), or stir-fried like regular fried rice (生炒糯米飯 *sahng1 chao2 naw6 mai5 fahn6*). Glutinous rice is opaque when raw, and turns into a gloriously sticky translucent pile that tastes heavier than regular white rice.

NOODLES

The options are seriously overwhelming when it comes to Cantonese-style noodles. A fantastic alternative when rice just doesn't do the trick, these strands of deliciousness come in all textures, lengths and thicknesses, and can be boiled in broth, used for stir-fries, and sometimes even deep-fried to a crisp. Cantonese noodles can be roughly split into two categories: those made with rice flour, and those treated with Cantonese lye water.

RICE FLOUR NOODLES
粉 *fun2*

Rice flour noodles are one of the most popular types of noodles enjoyed by Hongkongers. These strands are a distinct translucent-white color — not surprising given their main ingredients of rice flour and water — and are sticky and mushy to the touch.

❶ RICE VERMICELLI
米粉 *mai5 fun2*

The rice vermicelli is a particularly versatile noodle, being equally tasty as a stir-fry or in soup. The noodle is needle-thin, and can be bought fresh or dried.

Rice vermicelli is not to be confused with cellophane noodles (粉絲 *fun2 see1*) made from mung bean, potato, or yam starch. Despite the English translation, Hongkongers do not consider cellophane noodles to be noodles at all! Rather, they are used as stuffing for spring rolls and dumplings, or as a key ingredient in a main course that is eaten along with a bowl of steamed rice.

❷ MIXIAN
米線 *mai5 seen3*

The mixian ("rice thread") noodle is a chewy, tube-y starch that figures as a contemporary, trendy ingredient to a bowl of cart noodles (車仔麵 *cheh1 jai2 meen6*), see our Local Restaurants chapter). The threads are more firm and bouncy compared to the rice noodle and the rice vermicelli, and slightly less absorbent. Mixian noodles are made with rice flour and gluten-free flour.

❸ SILVER NEEDLE NOODLE
銀針粉 *un4 jum1 fun2*

The silver needle noodle is not a common dish for Hong Kong's younger crowd, but it's still a hot-selling product for the older generation. The silver needle is especially recognizable for its short length and pointy ends. A typical way of cooking this noodle is by stir-frying it with bean sprouts and shredded meat.

❹ RICE NOODLE
河粉 *haw2 fun2*

You'll encounter thick, flat wok-fried rice noodles (炒河粉 *chao2 haw2 fun2*) in local diners and Cantonese restaurants across the city. You can "dry-fry" (乾炒 *gawn1 chao2*) the noodles using oil and seasoning, or you can cook them in a thick, starchy sauce. There is also a thinner version of the rice noodle called soup rice noodle (湯河粉 *tawng1 haw2 fun2*), about half the thickness of the traditional rice noodle, that is particularly tasty when served in broth. Both types can be bought fresh at the wet markets or noodle shops. You can also find dried, packaged varieties at the supermarket, but buyer be warned: the differences in taste are astounding — the dried version doesn't even come close! Rice noodles are made with rice flour, gluten-free flour, and corn flour.

❺ LAI FUN
瀨粉 *lye6 fun2*

Very similar in shape, size and color to the rice thread noodle — except a bit more snappy and transparent — the lai fun is usually paired with a roast meat like barbecued pork or roast goose leg, and served in a clear, simply seasoned soup. Lai fun consists of a mixture of rice flour and corn flour.

LYE WATER NOODLES
鹼水麵
gahn2 sui2 meen6

There are noodles, then there are lye water noodles. An undeniable hallmark of Cantonese strands, most (non-rice-flour) noodles will have been treated to either a bit or a lot of Cantonese lye water — a food-grade, salt-based potassium carbonate and baking soda solution — during the manufacturing process. These noodles are typically yellow in color: a result of the chemical reaction between the alkaline solution and the ingredients in the noodles. Lye water helps preserve the noodles and gives them a crisp, chewy resilience. Lye water noodles are typically made with wheat flour and water, sometimes with eggs beaten into the mix. There are a few rare exceptions of yellow-colored Cantonese noodles where only flour, water and eggs are used; the vast majority would have been treated to lye water at some stage. Most good restaurants serving lye water noodles would boast that they've cooked them so well you wouldn't be able to taste the lye water — and thank goodness, because lye water tastes soapy and chlorine-like, and in high concentration can give the noodles a very distinct and not-quite-pleasant flavor. The secret to getting rid of the lye water taste? Remember to rinse the noodles in cold water after cooking, and to let the noodles sit for a while, allowing the lye water to evaporate.

❻ OIL NOODLE
油麵 *yau4 meen6*

Oil noodles are tube-y yellow strands that are a popular choice at cart noodle shops (see Local Restaurants chapter) around the city. They are relatively thick and bouncy and bode well in soup as well as in a dry sauce mix. Oil noodles are sold fresh at wet markets and specialty noodle shops.

THICK / THIN NOODLE
粗 / 幼麵 *cho1 / yau3 meen6*

❼ Thick (粗麵 *cho1 meen6*) and ❽ thin (幼麵 *yau3 meen6*) noodles are quintessentially Cantonese. Thin noodles are shaped like sewing threads, and thick noodles are pressed flat, its width about the length of a Japonica rice kernel. The noodles are springy in texture and very versatile: you can cook them in soup, stir-fry them, or even deep-fry them to a crisp. You can buy them fresh or dried. One variant of the thick / thin noodle is the ❾ wonton noodle (雲吞麵 *wun4 tun1 meen6*), typically made with duck eggs instead of chicken eggs for a thicker texture, and containing a higher-than-normal concentration of Cantonese lye water for extra crispness. The wonton noodle is a type of "raw noodle" (生麵 *sahng1 meen6*). The term can technically describe any form of uncooked noodle, but it is oftentimes used interchangeably with wonton noodle.

DRIED NOODLE CAKES
乾麵 *gawn1 meen6*

Dried noodle cakes are just as popular as fresh noodles in Hong Kong. Dried noodles keep longer, and are easy to store.

---

⑨ SHRIMP ROE NOODLE
蝦子麵 *hah1 jee2 meen6*

Invented around the 1950s, shrimp roe noodles have become quite popular in Hong Kong — partially because they are sold dried and can last for a long time without refrigeration. Shrimp roe noodles are thick or thin lye water noodles infused with tiny dots of savory shrimp roe. Different manufacturers will have different recipes for their noodles, and higher-quality ones won't add any artificial preservatives to their products. In terms of preparation, all you need to do is plop the noodles into a pot of boiling water: the noodles contain enough flavor to turn the water into a legitimately tasty broth.

⑪ INSTANT NOODLE
即食麵 *jick1 sick6 meen6*

Hongkongers love all things quick and easy, and instant noodles readily fit the bill. Although instant noodles can be loosely defined as any type of dried noodle that can be cooked by boiling in water, there are two specific instant noodle brands in the market that reign supreme in Hongkongers' hearts. Doll ramen noodles (公仔麵 *gohng1 jai2 meen6*) and Demae Iccho ramen noodles (出前一丁 *chuht1 cheen4 yutt1 ding1*) can be found at every self-respecting cha chaan teng and home kitchen. Both brands fall under Nissin, a Japanese foods company founded by the late Momofuku Ando, who was the inventor of the very idea of the instant noodle. The noodles first made their way to Hong Kong shores in the 1960s, and have since become so popular that they are now inextricably intertwined with Hong Kong food culture.

⑩ YI MEIN
伊麵 *yee1 meen6*

Yi mein noodles are always sold dried, in flat cylindrical yellow stacks that have been deep-fried beforehand. The noodles become a totally different entity once dropped in boiling water: they soften up, shed their greasy yellow color, and turn into wobbly, velvety strands. Yi mein noodles are typically turned into a sauce-drenched stir-fried noodle dish (after the boiling water treatment), and are occasionally cooked in a thick stew. Yi mein is a type of lye water noodle.

WONTON DUMPLINGS
雲吞 *wun4 tun1*

Although not technically a noodle, the wonton dumpling is another flour-based product that has become eponymous with Cantonese cuisine. The thin, velvety-smooth dumpling skins are made from wheat flour and eggs and treated with Cantonese lye water, giving them a distinct yellow color that sets them apart from the white, eggless dumpling skins of northern China. The dumplings are stuffed with pork and prawns, and are usually cooked in a seafood-based broth. They can be eaten on their own, or accompanied by thick or thin lye water noodles. Traditional wonton dumplings are small in size. The dumpling skins' square shape and the particular way the dumplings are folded, make the dumplings look like fluffly little money bags when cooked.

THE GRAINS OF TIME

Shing Hing Tai rice shop at Shek Kip Mei Estate has been around since 1971 and was opened by the father of current proprietor Wong Tak-kam.

Today, Wong still sorts his rice for impurities by manually pouring the kernels down a specialty chute, and sells the products straight from rice sacks rather than fancy packages. His type of shop, which requires quite a bit of manual labor, is slowly disappearing from mainstream society.

"All of the shop's rice is sourced from rice distributors on Hong Kong island and we only sell good-quality rice from Thailand," Wong tells us. "We don't sell cheaper rice. We sell medium- to high-priced rice such as Golden Phoenix rice (金鳳米 *gum1 fohng2 mai5*), a jasmine grain from Thailand."

"There is new rice and there is old rice. You need a sifu to blend the rice to get the perfect texture."

Wong Tak-kam, owner of Shing Hing Tai (成興泰糧食 *sing4 hing1 tye3 lurng4 sick6*)

When it comes to the different styles of rice, Wong says, "There is new rice and there is old rice. You need a sifu (expert) to blend the rice to get the perfect texture. New rice, which is rice that has been most recently harvested, is softer but has more of that distinctive rice smell. Old rice, which is rice from last season, is harder and has lost most of that aroma. Rice shops in the past had one sifu dedicated to blending old and new rice."

Wong has some tips on how to cook different types of rice products. "If you like your congee to be softer, use 'October rice ' (十月米 *sup6 yute6 mai5*). That's rice that had been freshly harvested in October, and is especially aromatic. If you prefer Chiu Chow-style congee, where the rice kernels are separated, [medium-grained] Australia Double Ram calrose rice (雙羊米 *surng1 yurng4 mai5*) is more suitable."

85

GOLDEN ROE

Gary Chan has been singlehandedly running family business Har Kee (蝦記 *hah1 gay3*) since the 1990s. The retail shop currently specializes in shrimp roe noodles and a few novelty-flavored varieties like mushroom and spinach.

"Har Kee Noodles began before I was born. The shop was founded in the 60s," Chan tells us. "For our shrimp roe noodles, you have to first and foremost prepare a good broth. We pan-fry some dried flatfish and boil them with some dried shrimp, to make a seafood broth. It's delicious. Then we add in the shrimp roe, which gives it a beautiful flavor."

"We then mix the flour with the broth," Chan explains. "The flour is a mix of strong [bread] and weak [soft] flour. Strong flour gives the texture and weak flour makes the noodles smoother."

"People are nostalgic for flavors of the past, so shrimp roe noodles have picked up steam again."

Shrimp roe noodles might be a trendy item these days, but it hasn't always been this way. "In the 90s, our shrimp roe noodle business was terrible," Chan says. "It was as if they had fallen out of style and become very outdated among the younger generation."

"Our business only survived because of our long-time customers. Maybe instant noodle companies had money to place bigger advertisements."

But time passed, and shrimp roe noodles became cool once more. "These few years, there's been a trend for simpler and more traditional things," Chan says. "People are nostalgic for flavors of the past, so shrimp roe noodles have picked up steam again."

Gary Chan, owner of Har Kee (蝦記 *hah1 gay3*)

HANDMADE STRANDS

Noodle maker Fat Kee (佛記 *futt6 gay3*) has been in business for more than 90 years, and is currently run by third-generation proprietor Nelson Law. Fat Kee makes most of its own products at a factory in Shau Kei Wan, producing rice flour noodles and lye water noodles for restaurants around the city. There are also several retail outlets offering fresh and dried goods to end consumers.

"My grandfather came to Hong Kong from mainland China and at first worked in one of the sampan restaurants [at the typhoon shelter in Shau Kei Wan] that served noodles," Law explains. "He made his own rice noodles and congee. He then opened his own noodle factory and restaurant on land. Fat Kee used to specialize in rice noodles, then slowly branched out to different noodles."

"Noodle machines made in Hong Kong are different from those in Taiwan and other [Asian]

cities," Law says, "because there is a bigger variety of noodles in Hong Kong. So while the noodle-making process can be more easily automated in other places, in Hong Kong we require more human labor."

At Law's factory, workers are employed to mix the dough, press the dough mixture into various machines, sort the noodles, and perform all types of other manual processes. Many of the workers have years of experience under their belt.

"Noodle-making is a funny business," Law says. "Even if the other sifu [noodle masters] and I use the same ingredients, the noodles we make will be different. I can give you the exact instructions — down to how long you should beat the eggs — and the noodles you make will be different."

> "Even if the other sifu and I use the same ingredients, the noodles we make will be different."

Nelson Law, owner of Fat Kee (佛記 *futt6 gay3*)

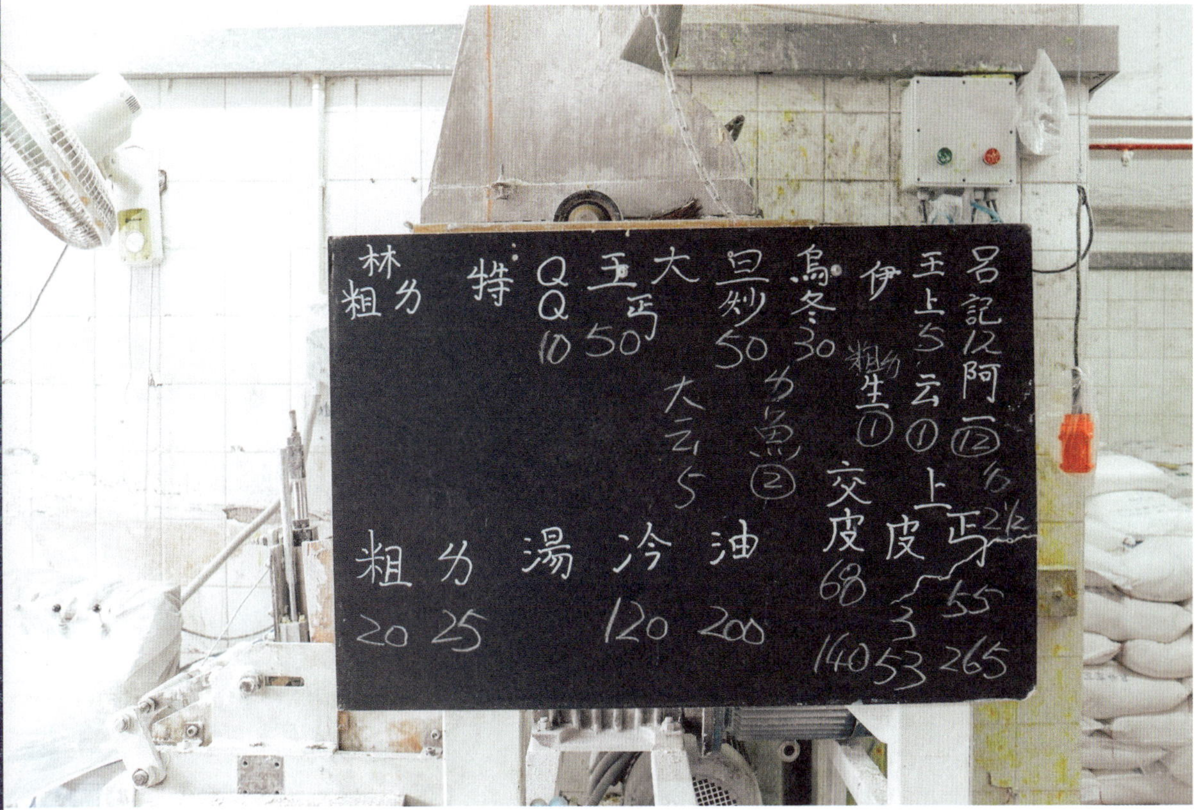
呂記12
阿一⑫
王上5
云①
上
伊
粗分生①
烏冬30
分魚②
大
大云5
王正50
QQ10
特
林粗分
交皮68
140
粗分
湯
冷
油
20 25 120 200

A LABOR OF LOVE

There's a humble little noodle shop in Cheung Sha Wan called Kwan Kee that specializes in a particularly laborious brand of strands known as jook sing ("bamboo") noodles (竹昇麵 *jook1 sing1 meen6*). It's a dying art, as it involves a human — usually a man — to bounce on top of a bamboo pole for hours on end to give the dough a springy texture.

"In my grandfather's days, the noodle's bouncy texture came mostly from duck eggs," says owner Mr. Lee. "The tradition of using duck eggs was just to give the noodles texture. But chicken eggs actually have a better taste. Now that quality high-gluten flour and lye water are available, I use chicken eggs for my noodles."

As to why he keeps the art of jook sing noodles alive: "I know for a fact that there are hardly any good noodles these days, and it's hard work to make truly delicious noodles. Making noodles by hand is 150 percent more expensive than by machine, and many business owners have opted for the more affordable option."

"Making noodles by hand is 150 percent more expensive than by machine."

Mr. Lee, owner of Kwan Kee
(坤記 *kwun1 gay3*)

"We make the flour dough by hand," Lee continues. "We turn the dough into a sheet using a machine. Our sifu uses the bamboo pole to press on the sheet about 10 times, then turns it 180 degrees, presses 10 times again, folds up the flattened dough, and repeats this process several times. This not only mixes the flour with the chicken eggs and lye water, it also reacts with the gluten and gives the noodles that bouncy texture. The machine then slices up the dough to make our wonton noodles."

"CLAYPOT" RICE WITH PRESERVED MEAT

臘味煲仔飯
lahp6 may2 bo1 jai2 fahn6

🕐 1 hour　　⏲ 1 night　　👥 4 persons

Claypot-cooked rice is a popular dish for the colder months. Traditional claypot rice restaurants cook the rice over an open flame for an especially smoky flavor — the charred rice bits on the edge of the pot are to cry for. This recipe tries to replicate the claypot rice flavors for the home kitchen.

INGREDIENTS

2 sticks preserved pork sausages
臘腸 *lahp6 churng2*

2 sticks preserved pork liver sausages
潤腸 *yuhn2 churng2*

1 preserved duck leg
臘鴨脾 *lahp6 ahp3 bay2*

5 pieces dried donko shiitake
乾冬菇 *gawn1 dohng1 goo1*

3 pieces conpoy　乾瑤柱 *gawn1 yiu4 chu5*

1 cup long-grain rice　秈米 *sahn3 mai5*

3 slices ginger　薑片 *gurng1 peen2*

Garlic slices　蒜瓣 *sune3 fahn2*

Granulated sugar　砂糖 *sah1 tawng4*

Chinese rice wine　米酒 *mai5 jau2*

Dark soy sauce　老抽 *lo5 chau1*

Scallion　蔥 *chohng1*

METHOD

1. Soak dried shiitake mushrooms in water-filled container, and let sit overnight. Place heavy plate on top of mushrooms to submerge the pieces.

2. Clean preserved sausages by using wet paper towel to wipe them. Don't rinse or soak sausages to prevent the casing from dissolving.

3. Rinse a cup of rice kernels and put into rice cooker. Add only 3/4 cups of water for an al dente effect.

4. Steam preserved duck and sausages until cooked, for about 15 minutes.

5. Rinse conpoy with water until soft and wet, and tear into small pieces. Smash ginger and garlic. Add ginger and garlic into frying pan, and cook until golden brown. Put conpoy into pan and add splash of Chinese rice wine and pinch of sugar. Stir-fry conpoy until dry and slightly browned. Dice shiitake mushrooms, preserved sausages and duck leg into small pieces.

6. When rice is ready, pour preserved sausages, mushroom, conpoy and preserved duck onto rice. Season with dark soy sauce to your liking. Sprinkle scallion pieces on top.

LOCAL RESTAURANTS

What makes Hong Kong such an exciting food destination is the fact that there are so many styles and types of restaurants to choose from.

CHA CHAAN TENG / BING SUTT
茶餐廳 chah4 chahn1 teng1 / 冰室 bing1 sutt1

Although there used to be more differentiation between these two types of local diners, today both the cha chaan teng and bing sutt tend to offer a similar menu of western-influenced Cantonese snacks and dishes. Traditionally, the bing sutt (literally, "ice room") offered cold drinks (which was a rather luxurious feature before the ubiquitous refrigerator) and snacks. The cha chaan teng — or "tea restaurant" — is believed to have evolved as a more sophisticated version of the outdoor dai pai dong hawker stall and the simple bing sutt.

The general gist: In the period after World War II, when the city was still a British colony, local restaurateurs started creating their own versions of western dishes to cater to the local palate, and at cheaper prices. The interiors of both the bing sutt and cha chaan teng are humble and no-frills, sometimes featuring foldable stools and tables as permanent furniture. Sharing tables with strangers is part and parcel of the experience.

For breakfast, sandwiches filled with scrambled eggs and either ham, spam or minced beef are an extremely popular menu item, as are instant noodles dunked in satay beef broth, or macaroni with slivers of ham in a clear pork-based soup. Lunch and dinner will see wok-treated dishes like fried rice and noodles make their appearance in a cha chaan teng, but some bing sutt nowadays will also carry the full menu. Yeung Chow Fried Rice (揚州炒飯 yurng4 jau1 chao2 fahn6) is a common cha chaan teng item: it's a yellow-colored rice dish that takes its name from Yangzhou province, where it originated. The rice gets its hue from the quick mixing of a raw egg into the rice while it's cooking in the wok. The Singaporean Fried Noodles (星洲炒米 sing1 jau1 chao2 mai5) is another cha chaan teng favorite: the dish consists of wok-fried yellow-curry-flavored rice vermicelli strands with bits of char siu and prawns.

In a bing sutt, snacks like Hong Kong-style French toast (西多士 sai1 daw1 see2) (deep-fried bread sandwich covered in an egg and milk mixture, with jam or peanut butter in the middle); egg tarts (蛋撻 dahn6 taht1) (a puff or shortbread pastry shell filled with a variation of egg custard); and "pineapple" buns (菠蘿包 baw1 law4 bao1) (a fluffy round bun with a crunchy sugar-topped checker pattern that resembles a pineapple husk) feature prominently on the menu.

Drinks-wise, the default beverage is a glass of hot black loose-leaf tea, served for free as soon as you're seated at the table. Some customers prefer to dip their utensils into the boiling drink for sterilization purposes, but this is more out of tradition rather than necessity. Most patrons will also order a cup of hot Hong Kong-style coffee, milk tea or yuen yeung (鴛鴦 yune1 yurng1) (coffee and milk tea blend) to go with their meals. In these cases, condensed or evaporated milk from the much-revered Dutch-owned Black & White brand (which landed on Hong Kong shores more than 70 years ago and has gained a fierce following since) is typically used in favor of regular milk. Lemon tea or sweetened lemon water, either hot or cold, are also staples. The branded Horlicks malted milk drink and Milo malted chocolate drink are especially popular amongst children.

Instead of dessert, many Hongkongers generally opt for an iced drink (冰 bing1) sweetened with sugar syrup or condensed milk. There are many variations, but pineapple, red bean, and salted lime are the more common flavors. A lemon coke (凍檸樂 dohng3 ling2 lawk6) — or coke infused with lemon slices — might not sound very exciting, but the drink is another local staple.

Some local restaurants cater to the late-night crowd, serving siu yeh (宵夜 siu1 yeh2) — or post-midnight snacks and meals — until the wee hours.

DAI PAI DONG
大排檔 *dye6 pye4 dawng3*

The dai pai dong literally means "big license stall" in Cantonese, which is an esoteric reference to the large-sized photo-based licenses given to the owners of such stalls. In essence, the dai pai dong is a streetside hawker stall that serves casual cha chaan teng and local diner offerings like congee, soup noodles and sandwiches; or seafood, claypot dishes and wok-treated options.

The traditional dai pai dong used to be much more specialized, offering only a few items at a time. A roast meat dai pai dong would be just that, and a dai pai dong that served sandwiches would not have also served noodles. But the lines have blurred over the years, and many dai pai dong stalls today offer a bit of everything.

Running a dai pai dong requires a special hawker license from the government. The government started issuing licenses to the family members of deceased and wounded civil servants after World War II to ensure they had a viable means of generating income, but stopped the practice in 1973, due to fears of unhygienic conditions and black market license trading. Most of the remaining dai pai dong stalls — 20-something in total — are concentrated today in two districts: Central and Sham Shui Po. This number will naturally decrease over time, as the licenses are only transferable to spouses or family members of the licensees, or not transferable at all.

Eating at a dai pai dong is Hong Kong's version of alfresco dining: customers chow down at makeshift communal tables while watching the chefs work their flaming woks in the outdoor kitchens. It's a tradition that Hongkongers are very proud of, and one that they are fighting to keep. Some dai pai dong stalls today have also taken over ground-floor indoor shop spaces to offer more seats to customers.

COOKED FOOD CENTER
熟食中心 *sook6 sick6 johng1 sum1*

Cooked food centers are restaurant stalls that can typically be found in the upper stories of government-run indoor wet markets. Don't be deceived by the dull-sounding name: cooked food centers often carry the same colorful dishes as those in a dai pai dong. Wok-fried seafood, meat stews, rice, noodles, poultry — different stalls might have different specialties, but the menu will usually be a mixed bag. Some daytime cooked food center stalls will also serve specialties that are similar to the cha chaan teng diner.

HONG KONG-STYLE FAST FOOD
港式快餐 *gawng2 sick1 fye3 chahn1*

Theoretically, most local greasy spoons offer fast food of some sort – you'd be hard-pressed to find one that actually encouraged diners to linger. But when it comes to fast food in the western sense of the word (with patrons lining up to order food at the counter), there are three dominant restaurant brands in the city that all Hongkongers are familiar with. Maxim's group, which has been around since the late 1950s, is one of Hong Kong's largest restaurant chains. Its massive portfolio includes a range of Hong Kong-style fast food establishments that sell rice, roast meat and noodle products the way McDonald's sells burgers and fries. Similarly, Café de Coral and Fairwood, two east-west fusion fast food brands that were founded by two brothers in the late 60s and early 70s respectively, take up a huge chunk of the local fast food market. Hong Kong-style fast food restaurant items include cha chaan teng specialties, soups, and some hybrid dishes like steak with Asianized sauces served on a sizzling iron hot-plate.

SOY SAUCE WESTERN
豉油西餐 *see6 yau4 sai1 chahn1*

Think of a "soy sauce western" restaurant as a Chinese-style western restaurant in Hong Kong, serving nominally western dishes that don't necessarily adhere to the original recipes and might feature some Hong Kong characteristics. The interiors of a soy sauce western restaurant resemble a western-style restaurant, typically featuring wood panel walls and booth seats.

Some popular dishes include chicken wings coated in "Swiss" sauce, which urban legend attributes to a mistranslation of a soy sauce and rock sugar-based "sweet" sauce; and saucy meat dishes served with rice (think "Portuguese" sauce chicken *(葡汁雞 po4 jup1 gai1)*. For dessert, baked souffle *(焗梳乎厘 gook6 saw1 foo4 lay2)*, sometimes in a variation called a "baked Alaska", is a common offering.

CHINESE BANQUET RESTAURANT
酒樓 *jau2 lau4*

The Chinese banquet restaurant — or "wine building" in Cantonese — is part of a group of hybrid Cantonese restaurants that typically serve dim sum (see Dim Sum chapter) during the day, and seafood and Chinese banquet-style dishes at night. This type of restaurant is also sometimes called a tea house *(茶樓 chah4 lau4)* or seafood restaurant *(海鮮酒家 hoy2 seen1 jau2 gah1)*, although their literal definitions have very little to do with their mixed-bag offerings.

The Cantonese tea house in its purest form serves only dim sum and tea, and only during the day, but these gems are very rare now as most restaurants that call themselves tea houses extend into dinner service. In the same vein, the original Chinese banquet restaurant used to specialize only in Chinese banquets — or multi-course meals for special occasions like weddings — although nowadays they are indistinguishable from the modern-day tea house.

There are typically anywhere between eight to 12 dishes in a banquet meal, and variations of the same staples almost always make an appearance. At weddings, this includes roast suckling pig *(紅燒乳豬 hohng4 siu1 yu5 ju1)* (which traditionally symbolized a bride's virginity but no longer carries such a connotation in the modern day) at the beginning of the meal. There would also be a lobster dish and a chicken dish, mimicking the mythical Chinese dragon and phoenix creatures respectively. The two animals are always paired together as symbolism of a married couple. Crispy chicken *(炸子雞 ja3 jee2 gai1)*, a deep-fried dish that consists of glazed, crisp skin and tender meat, is a well-known banquet offering, and a true test of skill for the Cantonese chef. The end of the banquet is typically signaled by the serving of both a rice and noodle dish, and a bowl of sweet dessert soup.

Chinese banquet restaurants are sometimes called seafood restaurants. Seafood is a precious commodity in Hong Kong, and according to some restaurant owners, this classification gives a more prestigious aura to a venue. Seafood dishes like marinated jellyfish strips *(海蜇 hoy2 jeet3)* (pictured), breaded crab claws *(炸蟹鉗 jah3 hye2 keem4)* and sea cucumber intestines *(珊瑚蚌 sahng1 woo4 pawng5)* (pictured) are examples of popular banquet orders.

Cantonese is a contextual language, and different words can sound identical to each other. Ingredient names can be twisted around to mimic a lucky phrase or theme. For instance, abalone *(鮑魚 bao1 yu4)* sounds like "full purse" *(包餘 bao1 yu4)* in Cantonese, and is a particularly auspicious dish to serve during Chinese New Year. (See Food for Every Occasion chapter.)

CANTONESE FINE DINING
高級粵菜 *go1 kup1 yute6 choy3*

Not everything is easy to classify, and Cantonese fine dining is one of those tricky categories. Technically, seafood and Chinese banquet restaurants are considered higher end than your local greasy spoon, but there are easily as many of these restaurants in the low- to mid-range tiers as there are those in the fine-dine spectrum. There is a definite subjective element in deciding which restaurants fit the fine dining description. Generally speaking, hotels are home to some of the city's fanciest, finest Cantonese establishments. There are also independent restaurant groups that have made a mark for themselves as bastions of Cantonese fine-dining. What they have in common: elegant aesthetics, exquisite plating and presentation, and an impressive bill to match. Each restaurant will boast its own Cantonese specialties, but there are common themes. Char siu made from the best cuts of pork, and a menu section dedicated to market-price fresh and dried seafood, are all hallmarks of a Cantonese fine-dine.

Dried shark's fin (魚翅 *yu4 chee3*), oftentimes boiled in a thick stew, has historically played a significant role in Cantonese fine-dining and banquet menus. It is viewed as a rare and highly prized item with a unique texture. In recent years in Hong Kong however, there has been controversy over industry shark-finning practices, and some fine-dining restaurants have removed the item from the menu. Dried abalone (乾鮑魚 *gawn1 bao1 yu4*) is another classic delicacy. In traditional Cantonese cooking, the abalone is rehydrated by soaking in water for days, then Chinese-style-braised in a thick sauce made from premium stock. The stock can be made from chicken, duck, or even spare ribs, and oyster sauce can be added to the mix. The slightly inferior canned abalone is sometimes used in lieu of the dried version. Dried sea cucumber (海參 *hoy2 sum1*) is also highly regarded, in part due to the intense preparation required to clean and treat the creature before consumption. Chinese-style-braising would be the default treatment on these bottom-dwelling slugs, which are rather bland-tasting on their own.

HOT POT RESTAURANT
火鍋酒家 *faw2 waw1 jau2 gah1*

Hot pot is a favorite Hong Kong pastime, and it's a particularly social activity given its communal set-up. Diners are seated around a shared pot of boiling flavored broth, raw ingredients are tossed in, and when things get cooking, it's all self-serve.

Hot pot restaurants in Hong Kong come in all stripes and sizes: they can be a humble hole-in-the-wall or a fancy venue complete with private rooms. Most hot pot restaurants offer a variety of soup bases, from plain chicken broth to fish head to spicy mala (麻辣湯底 *mah4 laht6 tawng1 dai2*). Common ingredients for hot pot include beef slices, fish and meatballs, leafy greens, and dumplings.

SEAFOOD RESTAURANT
海鮮酒家 *hoy2 seen1 jau2 gah1*

Seafood is a Cantonese specialty, and seafood restaurants in Hong Kong are a common sight. Many of them can be found in clusters in seafood-centric districts like Cheung Chau, Sai Kung, Lei Yue Mun and Lau Fau Shan, where they partner with retail seafood stalls located close by. Patrons would first purchase the seafood from the retailers, then bring the catch to the restaurant with instructions on how to cook each item. There are standard, textbook ways of preparing particular types of seafood. For instance, clams would be wok-fried with black bean sauce, fish would be steamed with soy sauce, scallops would be steamed with garlic and topped with vermicelli, prawns would be poached, and mantis prawns and squid would be battered and deep-fried with a five-spiced-based salt-pepper seasoning mix *(椒鹽 jiu1 yeem4)*.

Flower crabs would be steamed with Chinese wine, while mud crabs are commonly subjected to typhoon shelter-style treatment *(避風塘炒蟹 bay6 fohng1 tawng4 chao2 hye5)* (deep-fried with golden garlic chips, chilies, spring onion and fermented soybean paste). Typhoon shelters are little havens along Hong Kong's coast where fishermen's boats (as well as luxury yachts, these days) take refuge from the storms. In the past, fishermen lived in their sampan boats and called typhoon shelters home, and some even hosted entertainment and dinners on board. The dishes made by the fishermen were eventually known as typhoon shelter-style cooking.

Lobsters are poached in clear soup, or — and this is the only treatment that doesn't sound particularly Cantonese — baked with butter and artificial cheese sauce *(芝士焗龍蝦 jee1 see2 gook6 lohng4 hah1)* and served atop a bed of yi mein noodles. It is said that this treatment, which resembles an Asian version of Lobster Thermidor, was invented in Guangdong province.

Seafood restaurants also come in the form of regular neighborhood restaurants. Many standalone seafood restaurants boast their own aquariums filled with swimming fish, lobsters and crabs to entice the diners.

ROAST MEAT SHOP
燒味鋪 *siu1 may2 po2*

Char siu *(叉燒 chah1 siu1)* — or barbecued pork meat — is Hong Kong's unofficial national dish. Strips of meat, made typically from pork shoulder or pork loin, are marinated with a five-spice and soy sauce mixture, skewered, hung, then roasted in a large gas or charcoal oven, and glazed with maltose (or honey these days) to give them a glossy exterior. The char siu of yesteryear was wood-smoked and acquired a naturally reddish hue, but a lot of the modern-day char siu rely on food coloring to achieve the same ruddy shade. Char siu belongs to a broader category of Cantonese barbecued goods known as siu mei *(燒味 siu1 may2)*. Roast suckling pig, duck and goose are all popular siu mei items. "White cut" chicken *(白切雞 bahk6 cheet3 gai1)* and soy sauce chicken *(豉油雞 see6 yau4 gai1)* are also lumped into the siu mei category, although no roasting is involved. You can identify a siu mei shop in Hong Kong by the whole birds and the various cuts of meat hanging on hooks from the ceiling. Siu mei is often eaten with plain white rice and accompanied by a scallion-infused oil condiment. Sometimes roast goose would be served with a bowl of soupy lai fun *(瀨粉 lye6 fun2)* noodles. Chiu Chow-style marinated cuttlefish *(滷水墨魚 lo5 sui2 muck6 yu4)* is another item that sometimes makes an appearance at siu mei shops, even though it is not technically a roasted product.

CHIU CHOW RESTAURANT
潮州餐廳 *chiu4 jau1 chahn1 teng1*

Chiu Chow restaurants offer a particular style of cuisine that originated from Chaoshan region in the eastern part of Guangdong province. Things like fish ball and beef brisket noodles, and sha cha sauce (a popular condiment for hot pots and some stir-fried dishes) are said to have come from Chaoshan, which encompasses the cities of Chaozhou and Shantou. In fact, Chiu Chow is the Cantonese pronunciation of Chaozhou.

A lot of Chiu Chow restaurants specialize in soy sauce-based, slow-marinated dishes *(*鹵水 *lo5 sui2)* that give foods like duck, geese, tofu and pork an intense and savory flavor. Other signature dishes include cooked oyster omelets *(*蠔餅 *ho4 beng2)* (which are similar to western-style omelets) and Chiu Chow-style congee, which is a more watery version of its Cantonese counterpart.

NOODLE RESTAURANT
麵家 *meen6 gah1*

For Hongkongers, noodles are just behind rice in terms of popularity — and the variety of noodles you can find here is overwhelming. The two major Cantonese noodle shop categories are the wonton noodle shop *(雲吞麵鋪 wun4 tun1 meen6 po2)* and the cart noodle shop *(車仔麵鋪 cheh1 jai2 meen6 po2)*.

Wonton noodle shops serve thin-skinned wonton dumplings and Cantonese lye water noodles (see Rice and Noodles chapter) swimming in a dried ground shrimp and dried flounder-based broth.

Cart noodle shops evolved from 1950s street vendors literally pushing carts to peddle their offerings. There are no such cheap and cheerful streetside novelties today, but there are specialist restaurants in their place. The restaurants serve a mishmash of toppings to go with strands like rice noodles or Cantonese lye water noodles. Fish, meatballs and innards are common toppings, and you can even choose from differently flavored soup bases like beef brisket or spicy mala.

Chiu Chow-style fish ball noodle *(魚蛋粉 yu4 dahn2 fun2)* and beef brisket noodle *(牛腩麵 au4 nahm5 meen6)* shops as well as Cantonese-style "Yunnan mixian" noodle shops are also popular in Hong Kong.

CONGEE SHOP
粥店 *jook1 deem3*

Congee holds a special place in Hongkongers' hearts. It's the Chinese equivalent of chicken soup, and is the go-to for those who are sick. It is also a popular breakfast and snack item. Congee is essentially a thick rice porridge made by boiling the rice in a large amount of water for a lengthy period. At congee shops, the congee can be had plain, or with ingredients like century egg, salted duck egg, beef slices, minced pork bits, and endless other combinations mixed in. A popular sidekick to congee is a stick of deep-fried youtiao 油炸鬼 *yau4 jah3 gwai2*, which can be dipped into the porridge. When congee is eaten for breakfast, it is usually accompanied by a plate of soy sauce fried noodles 炒麵 *chao2 meen6*.

DESSERT / DESSERT SOUP RESTAURANT
甜品／糖水鋪 *teem4 bun2 / tawng4 sui2 po2*

Cantonese desserts come in many different shapes, sizes and textures, but generally speaking they can be classified as either solid or liquid form. Solid desserts include tarts, puddings, jellies and pastries, while liquid desserts are soups and pastes that are served hot or cold. Although you can find some of the desserts in regular Cantonese restaurants, there are also specialized dessert and dessert soup shops that only serve the sweet stuff.

Mango pudding, which is an opaque gelatinous affair, is an extremely popular treat found in dim sum restaurants or specialty dessert shops. You'll also find various jelly-like cubes flavored with everything from osmanthus petals and goji berries (桂花杞子糕 *gwai3 fah1 gay2 jee2 go1*), to sesame (芝麻糕 *jee1 mah4 go1*), to jujubes (紅棗糕 *hohng4 jo2 go1*), on the dessert menus of many Cantonese restaurants.

There are also the Japanese mochi-like treats, made from glutinous rice flour and filled with everything from peanut butter (花生糯米糍 *fah1 sung1 naw6 mai5 chee4*) to fresh mangoes (芒果糯米糍 *mawng4 gwaw2 naw6 mai5 chee4*).

On the dessert soup (糖水 *tawng4 sui2*) side, the variations are pretty much endless. Dedicated dessert soup restaurants serve everything from thick ground-almond paste (杏仁糊 *hung6 yun4 woo2*); sesame paste (芝麻糊 *jee1 mah4 woo2*); and walnut paste (合桃露 *hup6 toh4 lo6*); to tofu pudding (豆腐花 *dau6 foo6 fah1*). Tofu pudding traditionally consists of tofu coagulated with a bit of gypsum powder (石膏粉 *seck6 go1 fun2*), served in a bowl of clear broth that's sweetened with sugar or syrup.

There are also slightly less viscous dessert soups like red bean soup (紅豆沙 *hohng4 dau2 sah1*), green bean soup (綠豆沙 *look6 dau2 sah1*), and sago soup (西米露 *sai1 mai5 lo6*). There are more fruity affairs, like mango pomelo sago (楊枝甘露 *yurng4 jee1 gum1 lo6*), which is a mango-based soup dotted with pieces of sago and pomelo. Some dessert restaurants have gotten pretty creative over the years, inventing all sorts of fruity, beany, and nutty combinations that pair phenomenally with ice-cream and fresh fruits.

Then there are the clear dessert soups made from a combination of dried fruits like Chinese dates, fresh fruits like snow pear, and even dried fungi. The dessert soups are usually sweetened with rock sugar (冰糖 *bing1 tawng4*).

Hongkongers also enjoy hybrid-type desserts like steamed milk custard (燉奶 *dun6 nye5*), steamed egg custard (燉蛋 *dun6 dahn2*), and double-skinned milk (雙皮奶 *surng1 pay4 nye5*). They are not quite as firm in texture as the puddings and jellies, and have a consistency closer to that of tofu. The biggest difference between the steamed milk custard and steamed egg custard is the absence of egg yolk in the "milk" version — they're both essentially a milk, egg and sugar mixture. The double-skinned milk, meanwhile, is a sort of elaborate variation of steamed milk custard, with two different layers of milk skin formed by steaming the milk mixture twice.

All of these desserts and soups can be served hot or cold, depending on one's preference.

BY THE SEA

"My father was an indigenous villager in Lei Yue Mun," says Stephen Law, owner of Gateway Cuisine seafood restaurant. "He used to be a quarryman in Lei Yue Mun, as early as 1949. But in 1976, there were the Leftist Riots and the quarry business was stopped because the government banned explosive materials. My father was forced to do something else, and seeing several seafood restaurants had opened in the area, he decided to open a restaurant here."

Law's father first tested the waters with a bing sutt operation in 1969, but converted it to a seafood restaurant in 1970 when it became clear that it was the seafood businesses that were gaining ground in this district by the sea. Over the years, the family leased out their space to other restaurateurs, but in 1995, Law and his brother decided to take over and start afresh.

The way it works in Lei Yue Mun and other seafood districts, diners need to first pick their own live seafood from the different stalls located outside the restaurants.

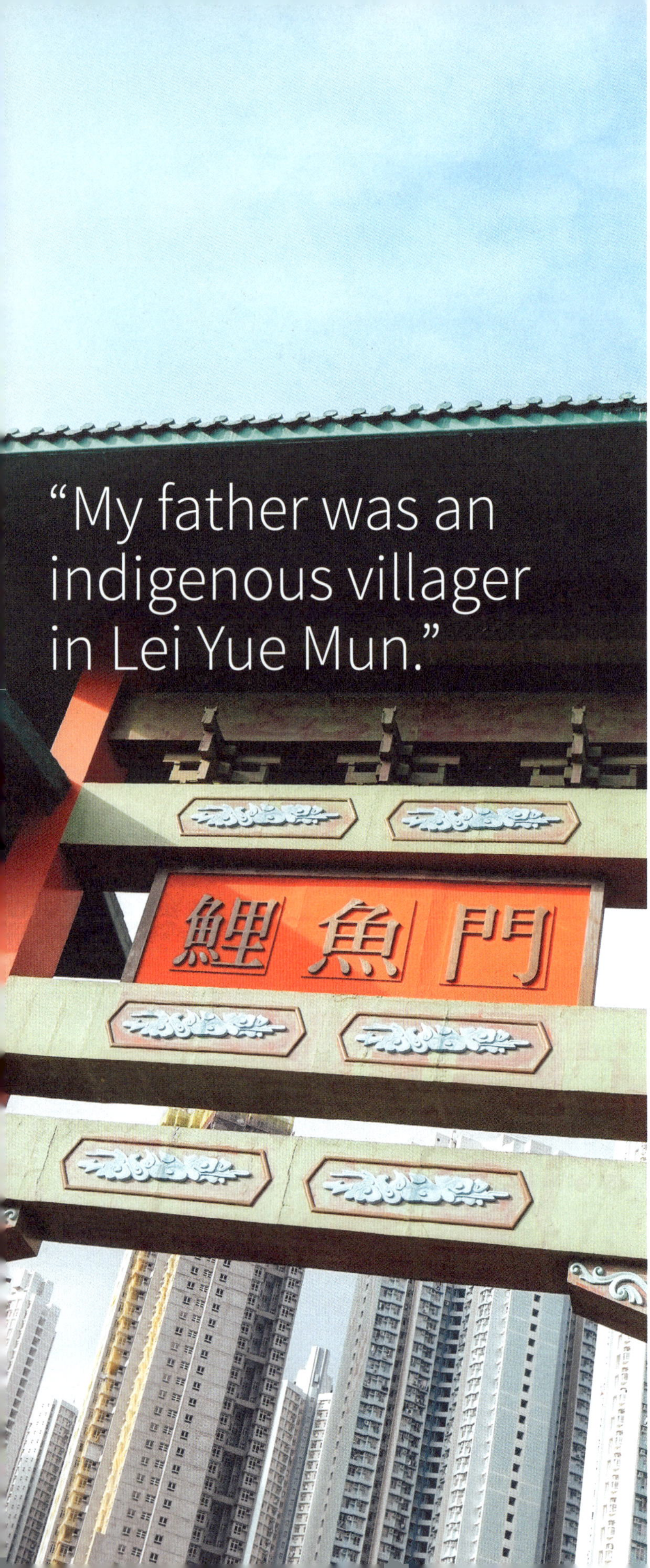

> "My father was an indigenous villager in Lei Yue Mun."

"The seafood stalls and restaurants are separated, I think, because it's more efficient this way," Law says. "The stalls provide the seafood and the restaurants don't have to hire people to acquire the seafood — only people to do the cooking."

"None of the seafood sold in Lei Yue Mun are from Hong Kong waters," Law explains. "Seawater in Hong Kong is heavily polluted, because so many people live here, and people don't dare eat the seafood caught in Hong Kong. The mantis prawns are imported from Thailand, Indonesia and Vietnam. The geoducks are mostly from Canada and America, the lobsters from Australia and New Zealand. The larger abalones are from Australia, the smaller ones from South Africa."

Stephen Law, owner of Gateway Cuisine Seafood Restaurant
(南大門 *nahm4 dye6 moon4*)

STREET SCENE

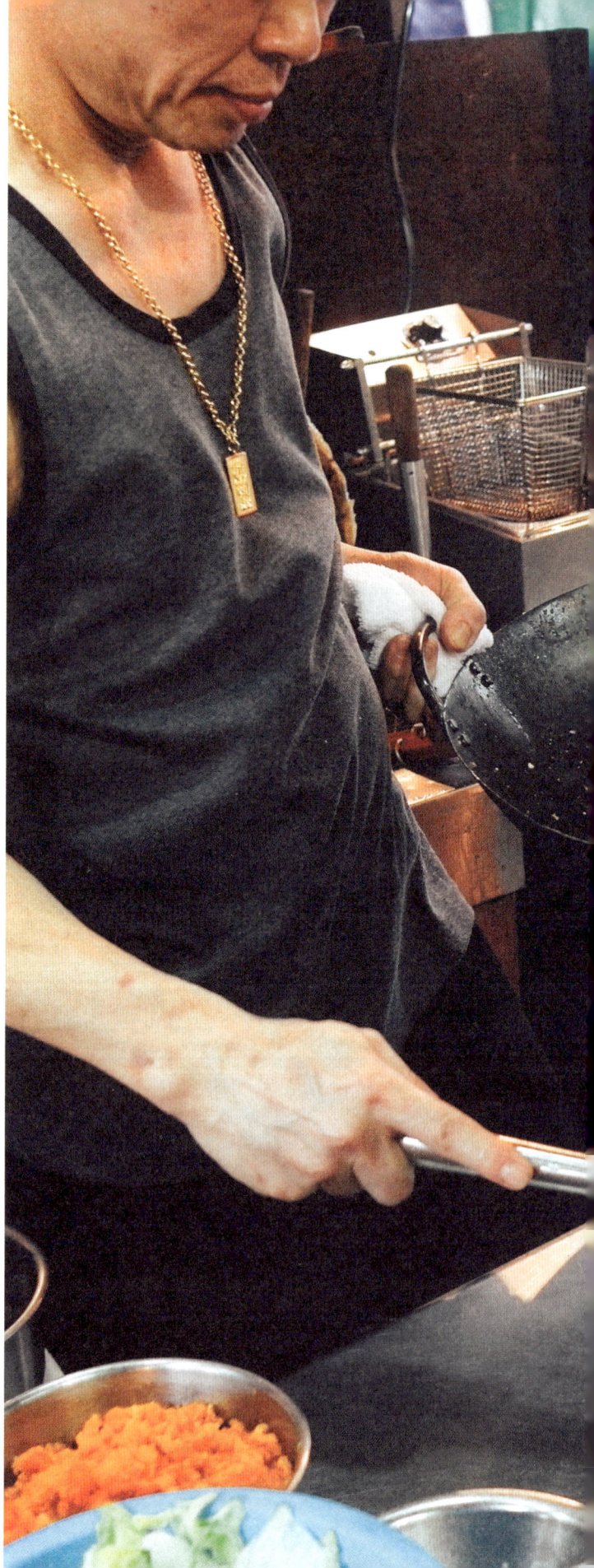

Oi Man Sang is one of the few remaining, officially licensed dai pai dong stalls in the city, and Wayne Wu and her husband Kenneth Lee are trying to keep the family business going for as long as they can.

The dai pai dong was started by the family matriarch, 80-year-old Mrs. Chan, who made her name selling roast meats at a small streetside stall. As business boomed, Oi Man Sang started offering wok-fried dishes and even took up several shop spaces to offer more seating.

Nowadays, Lee (Chan's grandson) and Wu have taken over the day-to-day operations. "When we first started in 1956, people just ate by the stalls, on a bench," Wu says. "As the dai pai dong became more popular, stall owners began to set up tables and chairs. Starting around the 2000s, more dai pai dong stalls moved into actual shop spaces. The dai pai dong started becoming more popular again, but the government also became very strict about hawker licensing."

"An open kerosene stove is really different. It's much stronger than your average stove and gives a unique flavor."

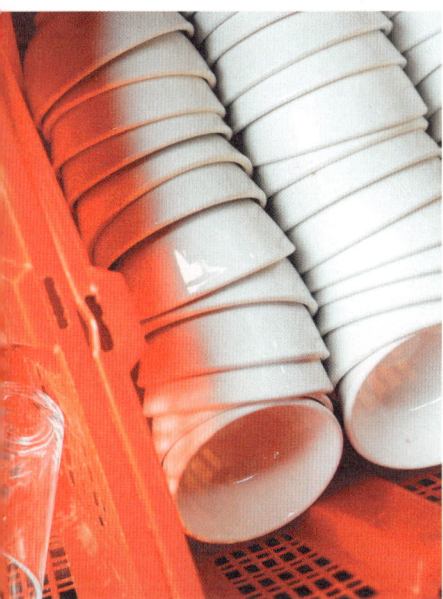

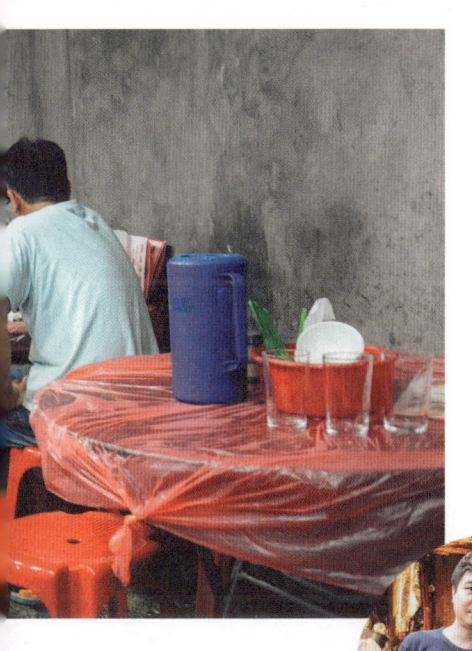

"We still use a kerosene stove," Wu says. "Many dai pai dong stalls and restaurants use gas stoves nowadays. An open kerosene stove is really different. It's much stronger than your average stove and gives a unique flavor. Its temperature reaches up to several thousand degrees Celsius. The second you add water into the wok, it boils. It cooks food much quicker, and gives a unique wok hei."

The original customers of the dai pai dong were working-class kaifong (街坊 *gye1 fawng1*) (neighbors) with blue-collar jobs. "We still have a lot of construction worker customers today," Wu explains. "They come here after work and meet up, sometimes bringing several bottles of Chinese wine. Then they drink until they throw up in our toilets. It happens about once a week. It may be a tradition among the industry."

Currently the government does not allow dai pai dong licenses to be renewed. "If the license owner passes away, you cannot renew the license," Wu says. "You can negotiate with the government, but it is very difficult."

Kenneth Lee and Wayne Wu, proprietors of Oi Man Sang dai pai dong (愛文生 *oy3 mun4 sung1*)

GOLDEN GOOSE

Kam's Roast Goose is a relative newcomer in the roast goose scene, but its recipes are age-old. "My family has been making roast goose for over 70 years. I've been in the industry for more than a decade," Hardy Kam, owner of Kam's, tells us. "My grandfather operated a dai pai dong. This was just after World War II. He started small and gradually expanded into the restaurant called Yung Kee, in Central."

"My concept for this restaurant is to focus on roast goose and meat — which is more like how my grandfather did it 70 years ago — serving mainly roast goose, char siu, chicken and marinated meat," Kam explains. "Some restaurants set up factories somewhere else to roast their geese, but for us, we want to do it the old way, and roast the geese in-house."

But not everything can be done the old way. "In Guangdong, restaurants still tend to roast meat using wood or charcoal," Kam says. "In Hong Kong, due to environmental and space concerns,

"We use a special needle to sew up the goose to seal the sauce, and then we blow air into the goose."

Hardy Kam, owner of Kam's Roast Goose (甘牌燒鵝 *gum1 pye4 siu1 aw2*)

the government has stopped issuing charcoal grilling licenses. So for newer restaurants like us, we use gas or electricity."

"Our geese come from southern Guangdong and are called domestic swan geese (黑鬃頭鵝 *hahk1 johng1 tau4 aw2*)," Kam continues. "They have long necks and are smaller in size. They have just the right amount of fat and fatty meat. They have thicker skin. For Chiu Chow-style marinated goose, a larger-sized goose is usually used."

The preparations can be tedious. "First we clean the goose, and stuff the prepared seasoning inside the body," Kam says. "We use a special needle to sew up the goose to seal the sauce, and then we blow air into the goose — people used to blow with their mouths, but now we have a device for it. Next, we blanch the goose in boiling water for about 10 seconds. Then we apply a sauce, a mixture of honey, malt and vinegar, onto the skin to season it and give it a nice brown color when roasting."

CHEAP AND CHEERFUL

Hing Kee might be a popular cha chaan teng on Hollywood Road these days, but it can trace its beginnings to a humble Sheung Wan dai pai dong from the 1960s.

"Hing Kee moved into this space about 24 years ago," second-generation owner Chan Chun-bun tells us. "Back in our dai pai dong days, we served mainly buns and sandwiches. Not many people could afford coffee and milk tea — they were luxury items."

But life on the street wasn't easy. "The government began to clamp down on dai pai dong, so we moved into a shop space," Chan says. "In the past, there was mainly the dai pai dong and there weren't many cha chaan teng shops. It wasn't until the clamp down on the dai pai dong that more cha chaan teng shops came to be. Back then, there were very few bing sutt shops as well. They were seen as higher class."

With Hing Kee's transition to indoors, the shop began offering noodles and more complicated dishes. But it has resisted adding wok-fried dishes like many of its counterparts. It has also kept much of its original menu intact, serving customers the same signature dishes for 50 years.

There's one special item on Hing Kee's menu that you won't see in many modern cha chaan teng shops: the boiled egg drink (滾水蛋 *gwun2 sui2 dahn2*). "It's basically water and raw eggs," Chan says. "You beat it and add sugar. It's a drink from our dai pai dong days. In the past, people didn't have much money to buy good food, so they'd order cheap and filling drinks like these."

Chan Chun-bun, owner of Hing Kee (興記咖啡室 *hing1 gay3 gah3 feh1 sutt1*)

SWEET TREAT

Rose Cheuk's desserts shop, specializing in tofu pudding, is one of Tai O's oldest. She's been keeping schoolchildren happy for decades, hawking her treats by yelling "dau foo fah" outside her shop after school hours to attract their attention.

Making the tofu dessert is almost an artform. "To start with, you soak the soybeans and ground them," Cheuk says. "Then you sieve the ground soybeans to squeeze out the paste. You boil the paste and add a little bit of gypsum powder — about a spoonful for an entire bucket."

Cheuk is a true artisan and uses her hands to do most of the work. "I grind the soybean using the stone grinder and sieve the paste several times to create the smooth texture," she says. "If you've tried a pork patty that was minced by machine, you'd find the texture mushy, right? The ones made by hand have a much bouncier texture. It's the same theory here. Using a stone grinder gives you a much smoother texture."

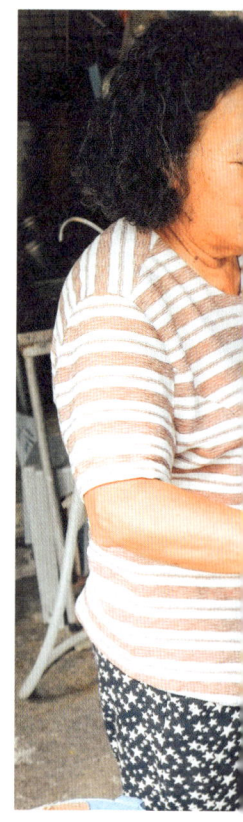

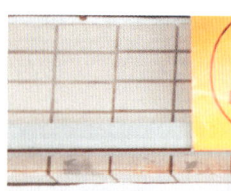

"It's the same theory here. Using a stone grinder gives you a much smoother texture."

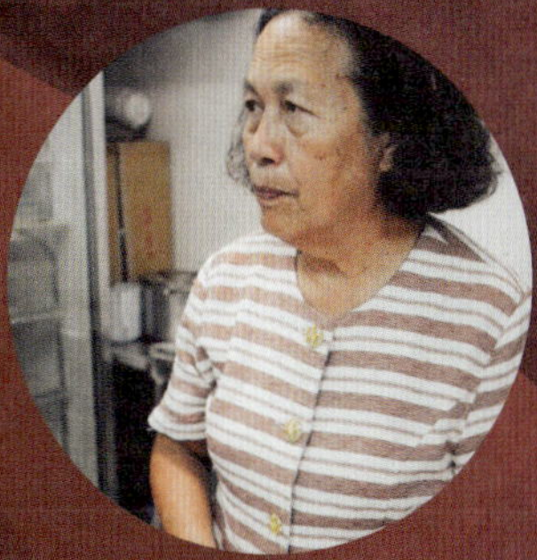

Rose Cheuk, owner of Station Tofu Pudding (車站豆腐花 *cheh1 jahm6 dau6 foo6 fah1*)

HOMEMADE CHAR SIU

自家叉燒
jee6 gah1 chah1 siu1

🕐 1 hour   🥄 2 hours   👥 4 persons

Roast meats are a rare home kitchen endeavor, because of the equipment, labor and time involved. But here's an unconventional recipe for a char siu dish that you can easily replicate without breaking your back.

INGREDIENTS

1 kg pork tenderloin 梅頭 *mooi4 tau2*
2 cloves garlic 蒜頭 *sune3 tau4*
1 slice ginger 薑 *gurng1*
Chu hou sauce 柱侯醬 *chu5 hau4 jurng3*
Fermented red yeast rice bean curd 南乳 *nahm4 yu5*

Chinese rose wine 玫瑰露 *mooi4 gwai3 lo6*
Honey / maltose 蜜糖 / 麥芽糖 *mutt6 tawng4 / muck6 ah4 tawng2*
Granulated sugar 砂糖 *sah1 tawng4*
Peanut oil 花生油 *fah1 sung1 yau4*

METHOD

1. Marinate pork with a tablespoon of chu hou sauce, a tablespoon of fermented red yeast rice bean curd, 2 cloves of smashed garlic, Chinese rose wine and ginger. Use fork to poke holes in pork multiple times to help flavors go through. Add peanut oil. Leave for at least 2 hours, and overnight for best effect.

2. Heat wok over medium to high heat. Fry pork until brown and slightly charred, for about 15 minutes.

3. Add enough water to cover about a third of the pork. Turn heat down to medium-low, and cook with lid on until sauce thickens. While dish is cooking, add sugar and honey / maltose to sauce mix. Serve hot.

WET MARKET CULTURE

It's true that Hong Kong is inundated with generic supermarkets and grocery shops in every corner, and is truly spoiled when it comes to access to internationally produced goods. But its traditional wet market culture is what makes the city unique.

Wet markets (街市 *gye1 see5*) are a cluster of grocery and fresh food stalls on the streets and inside government-owned buildings, selling live produce as well as fresh vegetables, fruits, spices and herbs. Wet markets are called as such, because the meat and seafood vendors typically clean their stalls by hosing them down with water. Outdoors, the water runs onto the streets and into the sewage system. Indoors, the water collects in grille-covered drainpipes built into the floors. Wet markets are a rowdy affair, and can be identified by their unique scent: a mix of ocean, fresh meat, and ripe fruits.

Each wet market is different, but you'll usually find stalls selling similar produce grouped together. Generally speaking, there would be a seafood section, a meat section, a fruit section, a vegetable section, and a dried goods section. Plastic bags abound, and it's one of the wet market's less attractive hallmarks.

You can also shop for dried seafood, pickled vegetables, fresh eggs, spices and herbs, and fresh noodles and dumpling skins at the wet market. Some of the more comprehensive markets might also host a stall or shop selling special branded sauces you can't find at the supermarket, like the popular Laoganma (老乾媽 *lo5 gawn1 mah1*) chili sauce from Guizhou province in southwest China. The wet market is also where you can procure Cantonese lye water (鹼水 *gahn2 sui2*) to prepare everything from zongzi (粽 *johng2*) to leafy greens (see Classic Dishes chapter).

The biggest difference between wet markets and supermarkets is that most of the produce in

supermarkets reside in a refrigerator or freezer, and only some live seafood might be kept in tanks, whereas at a wet market, you'll be able to find live or chilled poultry, live seafood, and non-refrigerated, freshly butchered meat and fresh vegetables. Wet markets typically also cater to the different seasonal variations in the region, while supermarkets can offer similar produce from all over the world, year round.

There are two terms you must get used to at the wet market: the tael (兩 *lurng2*), and the catty (斤 *gun1*). One tael is roughly equal to 37.8 grams, while one catty is equal to 600 grams. These two measurements are used for weighing many of the fruits and vegetables, meat, seafood and other miscellaneous items.

The produce at wet markets can be imported from countries around the world, but most will come from China, Southeast Asia and close-by nations like Japan and Korea. The live poultry and fresh meat are either from China or local farms based in the New Territories. The organic movement is slowly gaining ground in Hong Kong, and these days you might notice a few farmers' markets hawking locally grown organic produce from Hong Kong's own New Territories district in the north.

Prices are generally more affordable at the wet market than at the supermarket, although it does depend on where the items hail from.

MEAT
肉 *yook6*

On the red meat side, pork stalls are typically the stars of the show. Pork (豬肉 *ju1 yook6*) is a much more common commodity than beef (牛肉 *au4 yook6*) in Hong Kong, and you'll find rows and rows of pork stalls at every wet market compared to the one or two beef stalls hiding in a corner.

The butchers arrive to work early in the morning and start disassembling whole pig carcasses, hanging the different body parts onto metal racks built on top of the butcher's table. Pretty much every part of the pig is up for sale, from the bones to the innards to the tongue.

You can ask the butcher to cut up the pork the way you like. Depending on how you want to cook your pork, the butcher can recommend different parts that are particularly suitable. If you're making soup — and Hongkongers do love their pork bone soup — you'll get a piece of meat with bone (豬骨 *ju1 gwutt1*) intact. You can also purchase strips of pure pork fat — or essentially unrendered lard (豬油 *ju1 yau4*) — which the older generation prefers to use in their cooking. For instance, lard rice (豬油撈飯 *ju1 yau4 lo1 fahn6*) accompanied by a bit of soy sauce is a very traditional home-cooked dish.

The beef stalls function very similarly to the pork stalls, and all have a dedicated butcher to deliver the right cut to the customer. Popular beef parts include brisket (牛腩 *au4 nahm5*) and shin muscle (牛展 *au4 jeen2*) for Chinese-style braising, and cheaper cuts are usually turned into thin slices for stir-fries.

It's important to note that in Cantonese cooking, there is generally no notion of consuming any meat raw, beef included. The assumption is any meat bought from the market will be fully cooked at home, and the rough way the meat is handled at the stalls reinforces this truth.

On the white meat side, chicken is hands-down the most popular option. Some wet markets still offer live foul, as pickier eaters swear by the superiority of fresh chicken flesh. The chickens are usually kept in metal cages and customers are welcome to choose their own bird. The unlucky chicken is slaughtered and de-feathered right away.

Chilled-fresh chicken (冰鮮雞 *bing1 seen1 gai1*) is another offering at the wet markets. This refers to chickens that have been slaughtered on the same day (or several days ago for less stringent suppliers) and are then sold chilled — they are the next-best option to live chicken. Customers can ask for the meat to be chopped to their liking.

Hongkongers love to cook their chicken with the skin and bones intact, and most parts — including chicken feet — are game. Dark meat is typically more valued than white meat for its flavor and relative tenderness.

SEAFOOD
海鮮 *hoy2 seen1*

The wet market's seafood section is easily the liveliest section — buckets and water tanks are filled with swimming fish, live clams, wriggling prawns and all sorts of edibles from the sea. Nearly everything is sold fresh.

Some of the fish are sold pre-butchered and de-scaled, while others are killed to order. The many varieties of grouper fish (石斑 *seck6 bahn1*) — or garoupa, as it's commonly called in Hong Kong — are the most esteemed by far. But the choices are endless when it comes to fish: take your pick of grass carp (鯇魚 *wahn5 yu2*), pomfret (鯧魚 *chawng1 yu2*), yellowfin sea bream (黃腳鱲 *wawng4 gurk3 lahp6*), red snapper (大眼雞 *dye6 ahn5 gai1*) (pictured) and tiny whitebait (白飯魚 *bahk6 fahn6 yu2*), just for example. Hongkongers love to eat their fish whole whenever they can, preferring to steam, pan-fry or even deep-fry their catch. Bigger fish are sold by slivers. Fish heads are popular for making broths and soups.

Prawns (or shrimps) (蝦 *hah1*) both large and small are another popular wet market item. If you visit early enough, the silvery-blue crustaceans should still be alive and moving about. The prawns are typically steamed or wok-fried whole, with heads and shells still attached to the bodies. Fresh wet market prawns cannot even be compared to the bland, frozen varieties found in supermarkets.

Then there are the lobsters (龍蝦 *lohng4 hah1*), crabs (蟹 *hye5*), clams (蜆 *heen2*), razor clams (蟶子 *sing5 jee2*), eels (鱔 *seen5*), squid (魷魚 *yau4 yu2*) and things you might never otherwise encounter. Most are kept alive and slaughtered on the spot.

VEGETABLES
蔬菜 *saw1 choy3*

Vegetable stalls in Hong Kong hawk fresh produce that tend to follow the agricultural seasons, so depending on the time you visit, there might be very different items to purchase. The biggest players are the leaf vegetables — Hongkongers absolutely adore leafy greens. The varieties available are truly spectacular, but there are some perennial favorites that are quite common in Hong Kong.

Before we start listing, do take note that Chinese-to-English vegetable translations are highly confusing — and one type of vegetable can be given a handful of different, inaccurate and downright misleading English names. But here goes.

Bok choy (白菜 *bahk6 choy3*) is a reliable mainstay, and there are different types, including baby bok choy (白菜仔 *bahk6 choy3 jai2*) and Shanghai bok choy (上海白菜 *surng5 hoy2 bahk6 choy3* / 小唐菜 *siu2 tawng4 choy3*). Bok choy / baby bok choy have white stems and wrinkly dark green leaves, and are mustardy in flavor; there's a locally grown version of baby bok choy called hok tau (學斗 *hawk6 dau2*) that is quite popular. Shanghai bok choy comes with crispy, light green stems.

Then there's Napa cabbage (黃芽白 *wawng4 ah4 bahk6*), which is long and slim in shape and looks like a cross between cabbage and lettuce. Napa cabbage has pale green leaves and white stems.

Gai lan (芥蘭 *gye3 lahn2*) — variously known as kai-lan, Chinese kale or Chinese broccoli, but resembling neither kale nor broccoli — is another common vegetable. Gai lan is a stocky bright green beauty with thick, firm trunk-like stems and long, slender leaves and tiny yellow flower buds sprouting in between.

Choy sum (菜心 *choy3 sum1*), which looks and tastes similar to gai lan, is another Cantonese staple. It's sometimes called Chinese flowering cabbage but again, forget that name if you want to keep your sanity. Choy sum also sprouts yellow flower buds that peak out from its leaves. The vegetable has a softer, easier-to-chew stalk than the gai lan when cooked.

Scallion (蔥 *chohng1*) (also sometimes called green onion or spring onion, although both names can refer to slightly different plants as well) and cilantro (芫茜 *yune4 sai1*) (also known as Chinese parsley or coriander, but we know the drill by now), two garnishes that are essential to almost every Hong Kong meal, are usually sold together or given out for free with the purchase of other vegetables. White-bulbed scallion (白頭蔥 *bahk6 tau4 chohng1*) is more common in the summer, while red-bulbed scallion (紅頭蔥 *hohng4 tau4 chohng1*) (or simply red scallion) surfaces during the winter months.

Daikon radish (白蘿蔔 *bahk6 law4 bahk6*) (also known as Chinese turnip, just because), snow pea shoots (豆苗 *dau6 miu4*), water spinach (通菜 *tohng1 choy3*) (also known as Chinese watercress, water morning glory or Chinese spinach), chrysanthemum greens (茼蒿 *tawng4 ho1*) (pictured) and amaranth greens (莧菜 *yeen6 choy3*) are more examples of common wet market vegetables. The best way to learn about everything available is to go and explore for yourself.

THINGS IN BLOCKS

There is a miscellaneous range of items sold in blocks and cubes at the wet market, including fresh tofu (豆腐 *dau6 foo6*), dried tofu (豆乾 *dau6 gawn1*), and coagulated pig's blood curd (豬紅 *ju1 hohng4*) (which tastes better than it sounds). There's also the popular Cantonese dessert, garass jelly (涼粉 *lurng4 fun2*) (literally: "cooling powder", for its inherently cooling properties according to Traditional Chinese Medicine) — which is black in color and made from the mint-like mesona chinensis (仙草 *seen1 cho2*) plant. All of these items start out as giant slabs on a tray, and are then sliced to order.

FRUITS
生果 *sahng1 gwaw2*

Fruits make up the most fragrant section of the wet market, and you can find everything from strawberries (士多啤梨 *see6 daw1 beh1 lay2*) to mangosteens (山竹 *sahn1 jook1*), mangoes (芒果 *mawng1 gwaw2*) and durians (榴蓮 *lau4 leen4*) all in one convenient location. Lychees (荔枝 *lai6 jee1*), longans (龍眼 *lohng4 ahn5*), snow pears (雪梨 *sute3 lay4*), Java apples (蓮霧 *leen4 mo6*), watermelons (西瓜 *sai1 gwah1*) and pineapples (菠蘿 *baw1 law4*) are examples of other fresh fruits available. Most fruit vendors will let you try a few samples before you commit. Almost none of the fruits are grown in Hong Kong; they are sourced from all over the world.

EVERYTHING ELSE

As mentioned earlier, you can also procure fresh noodles, fresh dumpling skins, fresh eggs, cured eggs, dried herbs and spices, dried seafood, condiments, sauces and even the occasional frozen goods at the wet market. It's a great and affordable place to do your grocery shopping, and frankly a thousand times more interesting than the homogenous supermarkets across the city.

GREEN THUMB

Mrs. Ng is at her vegetable stall at the Shui Wo Street Market in Kwun Tong every morning by 7am, and doesn't rest until 6pm, when she closes shop for the day. She has been running her business since 1988, following in her father's footsteps.

"My father used to sell vegetables in a push cart. He didn't have a hawker's license, so we often had to run if the inspectors came. My worst fear was getting caught," Ng tells us. "I had a really loud voice, so I was usually the one who yelled, 'run ah!' (走鬼啊 *jau2 gwai2 ah3*) to warn the other illegal vendors that the inspectors were here."

Ng says choy sum is the best-selling vegetable. "Choy sum is very popular. It's in season throughout the year," she explains. "If you buy choy sum, I will hand out free scallion. People who buy choy sum here are usually regulars."

"In the summer, amaranth greens and water spinach are in season," Ng says. "Gai lan are available throughout the year, but they're not as popular as the other vegetables, maybe because they're harder to chew and the elderly don't have the jaw strength to bite through them."

"If you buy choy sum, I will hand out free scallion."

Mrs. Ng, owner of Shui Wo Street Market (瑞和街街市 *sui6 waw4 gye1 gye1 see5*) stall

SURGICAL PRECISION

"Being a butcher takes a lot of skill," Mr. Leung, owner of Loy Kee pork stall at the Shui Wo Street Market, tells us. "It's like being a surgeon. You have to have stable hands and be very precise. The meat should look smooth, without any flaws, so that customers are satisfied with the cuts. You also have to cut away the fat and tendons, so the meat doesn't look too fatty. People don't like fatty meat nowadays."

Leung sources his pigs from mainland China and Hong Kong, and the animals can weigh up to 96 kilograms. He sells two to three whole pigs per day. "It takes about 40 minutes to cut up a pig, but that's only if you are highly skilled," he explains. "It can take hours, depending on the person. It takes talent to be a good butcher. I started out late and, to be honest, I'm not a natural."

"It takes about 40 minutes to cut a pig, but that's only if you are highly skilled."

Being a butcher isn't the most glamorous job in the world, but that's never stopped Leung. "I don't mind being called a pork man (豬肉佬 *ju1 yook6 lo2*) at all," Leung says. "It's not demeaning to me, because that's who I am! I prefer being a butcher over being a cook, actually. I hate going inside the kitchen. It's full of oil and smoke — it's much more intolerable than being a butcher to me. Being a butcher is not unhygienic at all. We are very clean. We replace our knives and chopping boards frequently."

Mr. Leung, owner of Loy Kee (來記 *loy4 gay3*)

STIR-FRIED GAI LAN WITH GINGER JUICE

薑汁炒芥蘭
gurng1 jup1 chao2 gye3 lahn2

🕒 15 min　　🔪 10 min　　🍽 4 persons

Gai lan is a popular leafy green found at wet markets all over the city. The vegetable pairs extremely well with ginger, as you'll find out by following this easy-breezy recipe.

INGREDIENTS

1 catty (600g) gai lan　芥蘭 *gye3 lahn2*
Ginger　薑 *gurng1*
Granulated sugar　砂糖 *sah1 tawng4*

Peanut oil　花生油 *fah1 sung1 yau4*
Chinese wine　酒 *jau2*

METHOD

1. Rinse gai lan and remove any flowers. Cut and separate stem from leaves.

2. Make 2 to 3 teaspoons of ginger juice by smashing a piece of ginger with cleaver then squeezing it. Cut 2 slices of ginger for later use.

3. Heat wok over high heat and add peanut oil. Add ginger slices into wok and cook until fragrant. Put stems of Chinese kale into wok along with ginger juice. Stir-fry stems — moving them from side to center continuously — until they soften. Add leaves into wok and stir-fry until soft.

4. Add sugar, Chinese wine, and a bit of water and place the lid on the wok for about 2 minutes. Serve the vegetables.

STREET
FOOD
CULTURE

From its humble beginnings as cheap treats sold by wandering hawkers who couldn't afford a shop space, Hong Kong's street food today is a diverse mishmash of unique offerings that have evolved along with the city.

Whether it's a skewer of curry fish balls, made-to-order egg waffle pastries, marinated offal, a pack of candied fruits or hot-out-of-the-oven egg tarts, Hongkongers are simply spoiled for choice when it comes to streetside snacks.

It is said that street food culture in Hong Kong really started flourishing with the influx of mainland Chinese migrants during the early decades of the 20th century — a side effect of the civil war between the Kuomintang and Communist parties that tore the country apart. The migrants, mostly of modest backgrounds, made a living out of selling trinkets and affordable treats on the streets.

These ad hoc vendors grew in numbers over the years, and the colonial government started issuing Itinerant hawker licenses in the 1970s to regulate the business. Fixed-Pitch hawker licenses were also given to those who operated streetside stalls at designated areas. The Itinerant license doesn't restrict the hawker to a particular area, but neither does it grant a designated space to the hawker, while the Fixed-Pitch license serves the opposite function.

The government hasn't issued new hawker licenses since the 1970s and has been actively encouraging hawkers to trade in their licenses or move into shop spaces rather than continue business on the streets. There are also very strict rules in place for the transferring of existing licenses. In short, hawker licenses are getting rarer by the year, and if regulations don't change, it will only be a matter of time before hawker culture — and street food, in the purest form of the term — becomes a thing of the past.

In fact, much of the "street food" these days is sold in proper ground-floor retail shops at the bottom

of commercial and residential buildings in every neighborhood, although occasionally, if you're lucky, you will catch a few brave hawkers setting up their temporary and not-officially-legal stalls on a quiet street corner. These hawkers might have a simple makeshift charcoal stove over which they grill a crispy rack of egg puffs (雞蛋仔 *gai1 dahn6 jai2*), or a more sophisticated cart setup complete with giant wok for roasting chestnuts and quail eggs.

A lot of the street food as we know it was created by resourceful grassroots Hongkongers looking for ways to repackage inferior ingredients like low-quality fish meat or unwanted innards into something palatable and worth selling. But whatever its origins, street food today occupies a special place in Hongkongers' hearts. The city is taking increasing pride in its rich culinary culture, and there is a collective nostalgia for the unadulterated traditions of the past.

It is totally acceptable to be eating on the streets of Hong Kong, even while walking. It's easy to understand why when you see all the edible options that continue to tempt passersby in every corner, all hours of the day.

To get a taste of all the amazing street snacks available, make your way to Temple Street (廟街 *miu6 gye1*) in Mong Kok (旺角 *wawng6 gawk3*), where stall after stall of food hawkers will compete for your attention. But don't worry: street food is not at all difficult to find in Hong Kong, and you'll come across a specialty shop or two on most major streets in the city.

SAVORY SNACKS
鹹食 *hahm4 sick6*

The variety of savory street snacks in Hong Kong is endless, but there are common themes. Curry fish balls (咖哩魚蛋 *gah3 lay1 yu4 dahn2*) have, over the years, become almost the definition of street food itself. A lot of the fish balls found in street food shops are made from a combination of fish meat and flour. A good fish ball is one that's full of bounce — the proper way to achieve this effect is to give the fish meat paste a good pounding before they are rolled into balls, although again, most fish balls you'll find on the streets today have been mass-produced at a factory. The fish balls are then cooked in a soupy, mildly spicy yellow curry sauce and served skewered or in a round styrofoam bowl. The yellow curry sauce can also be used to cook pork rind (豬皮 *ju1 pay4*), daikon radish (蘿蔔 *law4 bahk6*), squid (魷魚 *yau4 yu2*), and pig offal (豬雜 *ju1 jahp6*), which are popular accompaniments to the fish balls.

The next most popular savory snack would be the siu mai (燒賣 *siu1 mye2*) — yellow-skinned fish meat dumplings that mimic the eponymous yellow-skinned pork meat dumplings you find in dim sum houses. There's actually not much variation to the streetside siu mai: most are procured from factories, and then steamed and seasoned with soy sauce and chili oil.

At some herbal tea shops and snack shops, you'll find marinated Chinese "tea leaf" eggs (茶葉蛋 *chah4 yeep6 dahn2*) (named after the Chinese tea leaf and five-spice powder-based broth they are cooked in) — which are said to have originated in mainland China.

Meanwhile, freshly made soy milk (豆漿 *dau6 jurng1*) and cifantuan sticky rice rolls (粢飯 *chee1 fahn6*) filled with pork floss and pickled vegetables, can be had at Shanghainese snack stalls around town.

On the fried side, there are the "Three Treasures" (煎釀三寶 *jeen1 yurng6 sahm1 bo2*) snacks where you can choose from a combination of pre-cooked items like fish-paste-stuffed eggplant, green or red pepper, red sausage slices and deep-fried tofu.

Stinky tofu (臭豆腐 *chau3 dau6 foo6*) is another popular street snack, although it's not particularly unique to Hong Kong. (The Taiwanese also love the pungent treat.) What gives the tofu its signature odor — which you can smell from a mile away — is the special brine that it ferments in. The brine usually consists of dried shrimp, curdled milk and some combination of vegetables. In Hong Kong, the marinated tofu is deep-fried in a wok full of oil and is then served with chili sauce.

There is a whole lot more out there, but things on sticks — from deep-fried pig intestines (炸大腸 *jah3 dye6 churng2*) to grilled satay meats (沙爹串燒 *sah3 deh1 chune3 siu1*) — sum up the savory street food scene.

PASTRIES
糕點 *go1 deem2*

Hong Kong-style pastries can also fall under the general category of street food. A lot of the pastries consist of an interesting take on western desserts and breads, due to the city's heavy colonial influence.

Egg tarts (蛋撻 *dahn6 taht1*) are one of Hongkongers' most beloved streetside treats. The traditional tarts, inspired by western-style pastries, consist of shortbread shells filled with a soft egg-based custard, although flaky pastry shells are also quite popular today. Fresh tarts are served hot, sometimes straight out of the oven. Egg tarts are a popular menu item in bing sutt diners and local bakeries.

Another heavy hitter is the bo lo bao (菠蘿包 *baw1 law4 bao1*) or bo lo yau (菠蘿油 *baw1 law4 yau4*) — literally, "pineapple bun" or "pineapple oil", which is a rather misleading name for the distinctly Hong Kong-style bread with unclear origin. Don't be fooled: no pineapple went into its making, and it's actually the pineapple criss-cross pattern formed by the crisp sugary crust on top of the fluffy bread that gives it its name. The "yau" in bo lo yau refers to the slab of butter that is inserted into the bread to give it extra richness (and calories).

Although not strictly street food, all of the other Hong Kong-style "western" breads (as they are so-labeled in Cantonese) that can be found in the local bakeries are worth a chapter of their own. These breads are typically sweet, glazed, and filled with ham, egg, sausage or cheese products.

Then of course, there are the egg puffs (雞蛋仔 *gai1 dahn6 jai2*) and egg waffles (格仔餅 *gahk3 jai2 beng2*), delicious airy "pastries" made to order in iron griddles. The egg puff batter is made from a combination of flour, eggs, tapioca flour and evaporated milk. The liquidy batter is poured into a distinct mini-egg-shaped honeycomb mold, where it cooks and sets, and is then peeled off the griddle and left cooling on a metal rack to allow the outer layer to turn crisp.

Some of the more creative snack shops will offer egg puffs in different flavors, like chocolate or green tea. The egg waffles are made from the same batter as the egg puffs, but are pressed into a more traditional waffle-grid mold. The result is a slightly denser pastry that can be folded up and filled with peanut butter, condensed milk, or even granulated sugar. It's hard to resist the treacly aromas of the pastries as you walk past the stalls and shops.

PUDDINGS, CAKES, CANDIES
糕點, 蛋糕, 糖果
go1 deem2, dahn6 go1, tawng4 gwaw2

The put chai ko (砵仔糕 *boot6 jai2 go1*) is not as popular as it used to be, but this sticky rice flour-based pudding, which is set in and gets its shape from a Chinese soup bowl, can still be found at some traditional streetside stalls and shops. The pudding can be made with white sugar or brown sugar, and the color of the end product reflects the ingredients used. Sometimes, red beans are also added into the pudding. The pudding is usually pried out from its host bowl upon purchase, and spiked onto two thin bamboo skewers for easy and hands-free consumption.

The fluffy white sugar sponge cake (白糖糕 *bahk6 tawng4 go1*) is another traditional Cantonese street snack made from rice flour and water.

Candied fruits (涼果 *lurng4 gwaw2*) are yet another nostalgic treat that can be found on the streets. Prunes (both with pit or pitless), lemons, tangerine peel (and even spices like ginger) are dried, then coated with sugar and other seasonings like licorice or salt. The candied fruits are sometimes displayed in giant jars and sold by weight, or pre-packaged into neat little bags.

Dragon's beard candy (龍鬚糖 *lohng4 so1 tawng2*) (a combination of peanut bits and coconut shavings enclosed by a cocoon of wispy white threads made from spun sugar) and deuk deuk tong (啄啄糖 *durk1 durk1 tawng2*) (a hardened maltose candy, sometimes served between two western-style crackers) are more snacks that will take you for a trip down memory lane.

SEASONAL SNACKS
季節小食 *gwai3 jeet3 siu2 sick6*

When the temperatures drop, roasted chestnut (炒栗子 *chao2 luht6 jee2*) hawkers come out in full force. They toss the chestnuts on to a giant coal-filled wok, stirring and stirring until the surrounding air becomes engulfed in a sticky-sweet aroma. Sometimes, tiny quail eggs get tossed into the mix. Sweet potatoes are another common companion.

In the summer, a cup of herbal tea (涼茶 *lurng4 chah4*) (see TCM chapter) or a bowl of grass jelly (涼粉 *lurng4 fun2*) is a refreshing relief against the sweltering heat.

SWEET TREATS

Tong Sung-chiu mans the Lemon King stall on Wing Kut Street in Central, just as his late father had done since the 1970s. The signature item for sale is the candied "lemon", made actually from preserved kaffir limes that have been sweetened in a white sugar solution.

"My father started as an illegal vendor on the streets, with a push cart," Tong says. "Before candied lemons, he sold many things, from ballpoint pens to preserved meat. Then he met a fellow street vendor who sold Cantonese preserved snacks. The vendor provided my father with preserved lemons. He processed and added licorice powder to the lemons, then started selling them."

At first, Tong had a difficult time trying to take over the business from his ailing father. "The hawker license belonged to my father, and as his

health deteriorated, he came out to the stall less and less," he tells us. "But people complained, and the Food and Environmental Hygiene Department came to inspect our stall — and because the license was not transferable, they charged us for operating illegal hawking activities."

It was only when a prominent local food writer highlighted Tong's plight that a new license was issued by the FEHD, enabling Tong to continue operations. To this day, the stall is very popular with new and old customers alike.

"I remember one time, an elderly man in his 80s came to our stall with a walking stick in his hand," Tong says. "I asked him where he came from, and he said, 'Very, very far away!' I thought it was the New Territories or one of the outlying islands, but he was from New York."

"He said he came to see how my father was doing. I told him that my father rarely came to the stall anymore," Tong continues. "I was really moved. After all these years, we still hold a place in his memory. He wanted to see how we were doing."

"The vendor provided my father with preserved lemons. He processed and added licorice powder to the lemons, then started selling them."

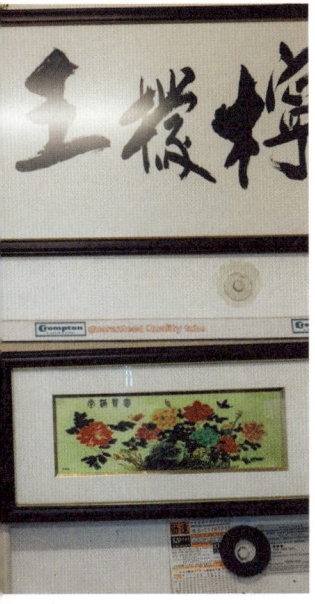
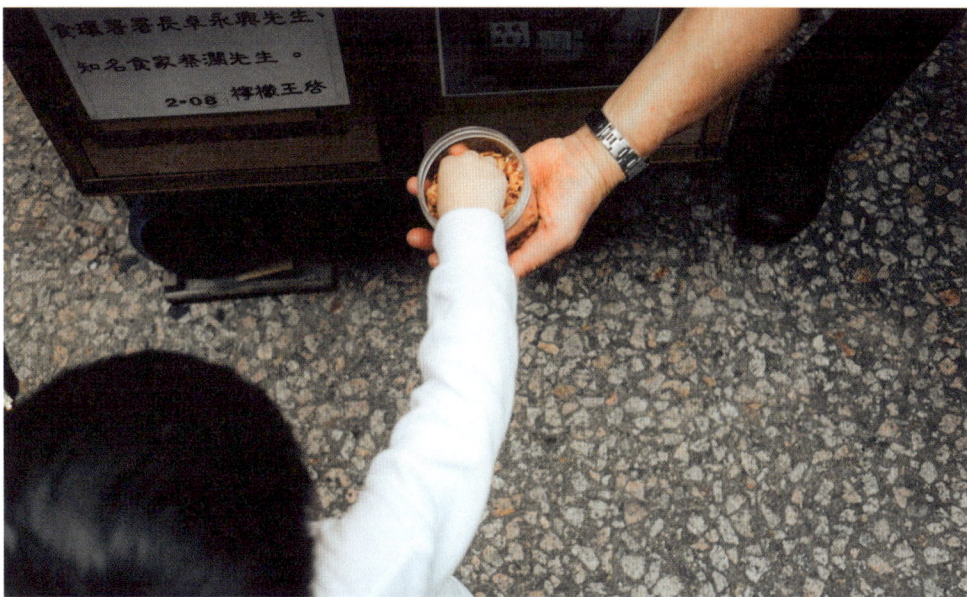

Tong Sung-chiu, owner of Lemon King hawker stall (檸檬王 *ning4 mohng1 wawng4*)

THE SQUID SQUAD

Mrs. Ho's father-in-law started out as a push-cart hawker in the 80s, selling snacks like fish balls and curry squid, before he eventually settled in a shop space in Wan Chai and christened it Chuen Cheong Foods. Mrs. Ho and her son Sherman run the streetside shop, which offers a much wider range of snacks.

One of the specialties at Chuen Cheong is the stinky tofu. "Stinky tofu has a long history, even longer than our hawker push cart!" Ho says. "In Hong Kong, stinky tofu is mainly deep-fried. One of my friends makes really good stinky tofu, and we started buying from her."

Besides the pungent snack, curry squid, fish balls, sea snail, and marinated pork skin and daikon radish are also very popular items. "My father-in-law began with the curry squid," Ho says. "Curry squid used to be available only at the herbal tea shops. My father-in-law decided to sell them on the street. You don't see them in street food stalls anymore."

"We make our curry squid from dried squid (土鱿 *toh2 yau2*)," Ho explains. "We soak them in water and some Cantonese lye water, and then marinate them for a day. We use dried squid because it packs much more flavor. Fresh squid doesn't taste the same. We make our own curry sauce, and then stir-fry the squid with the sauce for about half an hour."

"We use dried squid because it packs much more flavor. Fresh squid doesn't taste the same."

Mrs. Ho and son Sherman Ho, owners of Chuen Cheong Foods (泉昌美食 *chune4 churng1 may5 sick6*)

CURRY IN A HURRY

Fish balls are ubiquitous on Hong Kong's streets, but not all fish ball stalls were created equal. Just ask Jason Lam, owner of popular fish ball chain Lam Cheong Kee. He started selling his own brand of curry fish balls at the Sham Shui Po Chinese New Year's market, and had amassed a loyal following from the very first day.

"To tell you the truth, there is no secret recipe to our fish balls," Lam tells us. "We use fish caught in local waters from the upper-middle depths of the sea. The fish balls are made fresh in the store."

"As long as you know which types of fish have the right texture and which types of fish have the right stickiness, you can calculate the proper ratios for the fish paste," Lam continues. "There are fish bones in our fish balls, but you can't taste them. It's been finely ground. Having bones in the fish balls actually makes them tastier."

As for the distinct Hong Kong-style curry sauce that goes along with the fish balls, Lam uses a whole bunch of different ingredients to achieve the savory, mildly spicy flavors. "I use Chinese sauces like sha cha sauce. The taste profile fits our Hong Kong-style curry."

Jason Lam, owner of Lam Cheong Kee (林昌記 *lum4 churng1 gay3*)

PAN-FRIED "THREE TREASURES"

煎釀三寶
jeen1 yurng6 sahm1 bo2

 20 min    15 min    4 persons

Pan-fried "three treasures" are found at street food stalls across the city. The main ingredient here is the fish paste, made from small but tasty dace fish.

INGREDIENTS

1 green pepper 青椒 *cheng1 jiu1*
Half an eggplant 茄子 *keh2 jee2*
4 pieces fresh tofu 豆腐 *dau6 foo6*
1 catty (600g) minced dace fish 鯪魚肉 *leng4 yu4 yook6*

Scallion 蔥 *chohng1*
Peanut oil 花生油 *fah1 sung1 yau4*
Salt 鹽 *yeem4*
Cornstarch 生粉 *sahng1 fun2*

METHOD

1. Put minced dace fish in a bowl and add a touch of peanut oil and salt. Pick up a palmful of minced dace fish, and gently toss into the bowl. Repeat until dace fish mixture thickens slightly. This technique adds texture to the batter and results in a more fluffy fish cake. Chop up scallion and mix into batter.

2. Rinse green peppers and eggplant. Cut green peppers into roughly 8 to 9 pieces. Slice eggplant into thick pieces, then cut halfway through the middle of each piece for stuffing with minced fish later. For the tofu, use a spoon to remove a bit off the top, making a shallow dent in the center.

3. Smear cornstarch onto insides of the green pepper. Pick up fish mixture using a spoon, and pile into green pepper. Repeat with eggplant slices and tofu.

4. Heat frying pan to medium heat and add peanut oil. Put stuffed vegetables inside pan, fish-cake-side first. Pan-fry until golden and flip over. When the ingredients char slightly, serve. Eat with oyster sauce and chili sauce.

DIM SUM
AND
TEA CULTURE

Dim sum (點心 *deem 2 sum1*) — typically a leisurely morning or early afternoon meal — is a favorite pastime for Hongkongers. Having dim sum is as much about enjoying the company of the people you dine with as it is about the food itself.

HISTORY

The social activity known as dim sum (點心 *deem2 sum1*) is in fact intricately linked to southern Chinese tea drinking culture. The Cantonese phrase: yum cha (飲茶 *yum2 chah4*) (literally, "drink tea") is used interchangeably with the term dim sum — which itself roughly translates to "pieces of the heart", and refers to the tapas-like small dishes that are served during a dim sum meal.

The practice of tea drinking originated in southern and central China in the Han Dynasty (206 BCE to 220 CE). Throughout the years, tea making evolved and different tea trends developed: tea leaves were boiled with spices; ground into powder and mixed with water; and even combined with cream. Tea was served in tea houses dotted along the ancient Silk Road to quench the thirst of weary traders and travelers.

Some time in the Yuan Dynasty (1271 to 1368), it became common to consume small snacks like nuts and seeds along with tea. These snacks eventually became meals in their own right, and dim sum was born.

In Hong Kong specifically, the first tea houses were established around the 1840s, offering fresh brews at cheap prices and snacks to go along. By the mid-1840s, the tea houses transitioned from simple shacks to two-story establishments, offering their goods at two distinct price points: the ground floor with the more affordable prices was reserved for the common folk, while the fancier upper floor specifically catered to the rich. Common accessories at each table included a spittoon on the ground, and a kettle filled with hot water for the ease of replenishing empty teacups. Staff

brought out the dim sum on trays that were attached to straps around their necks.

Gradually, some of the fancier tea houses were said to have adopted a Guangdong-style decor, which included mahogany furniture and colorfully stained windows. Starting from the 1950s, tea houses became multi-functional, offering meals as well as mahjong rooms and banquet facilities.

Around the 1970s, the tables at some of the tea houses had glass tops and a shallow compartment underneath, allowing diners to enjoy hot dim sum dishes first, while stowing chilled and sweet dishes below for later consumption.

Customers were also able to order their dim sum from moving push carts, also known as trolleys, pointing to the steamed baskets they wanted and having staff transfer the dishes to the table. Fast forward to today, and this practice has become increasingly rare. Delivery by trolley is inefficient, and tea houses have downsized, thanks to Hong Kong's preciously high property prices and rents. These days, taking your pick of dishes from an order sheet provided on the table is a much more likely scenario.

In modern times, dim sum is not restricted to being served at specialty dim sum establishments. Dim sum can be found at tea houses (茶樓 *chah4 lau4*), Chinese banquet restaurants (酒樓 *jau2 lau4*) and even seafood restaurants (海鮮酒家 *hoy2 seen1 jau2 gah1*) (see Local Restaurants chapter).

THE HONG KONG WAY

Dim sum can be a big-group or lone-wolf affair: you're just as likely to see families take over an entire round table, as you are a gentleman chowing down on his own, newspaper in hand.

Regardless of the size of the parties present, any respectable dim sum hall would be a buzzing environment, filled with chatter and roaming staff. Dim sum is a highly social activity — even if you're eating alone, there's nothing stopping you from talking to your neighbors or even sharing a table with complete strangers.

At some dim sum halls, dim sum is available in the early mornings. For the masses, 11am to 2pm is the generally accepted timeframe to tuck in. These days, however, you'll be able to find a dim sum shop that's open no matter what time you're craving it, and having dim sum for dinner or a late-night snack isn't nearly as strange as it would've been in the past.

Some of the older or more traditional dim sum restaurants would provide diners with a giant bowl of hot tea to wash their utensils, plates, and bowls in. The idea is that the boiling-hot tea would kill any bacteria or rinse away any unclean spots. Today, this practice sometimes feels more like lingering tradition than an official sanitizing procedure.

When ordering, dim sum dishes can typically be categorized under different sizes (like small, medium, and large), each with a corresponding price point attached.

TEA

Dim sum is a tradition that evolved straight out of the practice of drinking tea, so no dim sum experience would be complete without a pot of tea to go along.

In Hong Kong, there are several types of teas that dim sum restaurants commonly offer (as shown below). With the exception of floral brews, Chinese teas are all made from the leaves of the Camellia sinensis shrub (which includes different cultivars, just like wine grape varietals). The treatment of the leaves (i.e. rolled vs. pressed) and the oxidization or fermentation processes also give the teas different colors and flavors.

WULONG
烏龍 *woo1 lohng2*

Wulong tea is actually a general term for one of the six major types of Chinese tea. Partially oxidized, it can take on different flavors depending on how it is made. Generally speaking, wulong is milder in taste compared to the heavy Pu'er.

PU'ER
普洱 *po2 lay2*

Pu'er tea is a type of dark, fermented tea known as black tea (黑茶 *hahk1 chah4*). It originated from Yunnan province in China, and the ripe variety is dark orange-brown in color and tastes quite intense. Side note: western-style black tea is referred to as red tea (紅茶 *hohng4 chah4*) in Chinese, and should not be confused with Chinese-style black tea.

SHOUMEI
壽眉 *sau6 may2*

Shoumei tea is a type of white tea (白茶 *bahk6 chah4*). White teas are generally made from young tea leaves that have been only lightly processed. Shoumei is strongly flavored, compared to other white teas.

TIEGUANYIN
鐵觀音 *teet3 goon1 yum1*

Tieguanyin is one particularly fragrant style of wulong tea. The tea is named after Guanyin, the Chinese goddess of mercy. Dark tieguanyin roasts were the norm in the tea houses of yore, but a lighter, more delicate roast is gaining ground with today's tea drinkers.

SHUIXIAN
水仙 *sui2 seen1*

Shuixian tea is yet another style of wulong tea. The tea is known for its sweet, honey-like notes and strong, dark color.

CHRYSANTHEMUM PU'ER
菊普 *gook1 po2*

Chrysanthemum tea (菊花 *gook1 fah1*) is naturally made from the chrysanthemum flower, and is typically stocked by the fancier establishments, but a chrysanthemum-pu'er blend is a more common offering.

Likewise, jasmine tea (香片 *hurng1 peen2*), usually presented as a green tea blend, is another popular option these days.

POPULAR DIM SUM DISHES

PRAWN DUMPLINGS / HAR GOW
蝦餃 *hah1 gao2*

SPRING ROLLS
春卷 *chuhn1 gune2*

STEAMED RICE NOODLE ROLLS
腸粉 *churng2 fun2*

DEEP-FRIED BEAN CURD SHEET ROLLS
腐皮卷 *foo6 pay4 gune2*

STEAMED BEEF BALLS
牛肉球 *au4 yook6 kau4*

STICKY RICE DOUGH PORK DUMPLINGS
咸水角 *hahm4 sui2 gawk3*

CHIU CHOW-STYLE DUMPLINGS
潮州粉粿 *chiu4 jau1 fun2 gwaw2*

MARINATED STEAMED SQUID
蒸鮮魷 *jing1 seen1 yau2*

PORK DUMPLINGS / SIU MAI
燒賣 *siu1 mye2*

BARBECUED PORK BUNS / CHAR SIU BAO
叉燒包 *chah1 siu1 bao1*

DAIKON "TURNIP" CAKE
蘿蔔糕 *law4 bahk6 go1*

STEAMED BEAN CURD SHEET ROLLS
鮮竹卷 *seen1 jook1 gune2*

STEAMED SPARE RIBS WITH RICE
蒸排骨飯 *jing1 pye4 gwutt1 fahn6*

CUSTARD BUNS
奶皇包 *nye5 wawng4 bao1*

DEEP-FRIED MILK CUSTARD
炸鮮奶 *jah3 seen1 nye5*

DEEP-FRIED SQUID TENTACLES
炸魷魚 *jah3 yau4 yu2*

LOTUS PASTE BUNS
蓮蓉包 *leen4 yohng4 bao1*

OLD-SCHOOL CHARM

Chui Kwok-hing is the second-generation owner of Sun Hing Restaurant, a decades-old dim sum brand. The restaurant opens at unconventional hours — from 3am to 4pm — each day, originally to accommodate the schedules of shift workers, but now attracting crowds of university students, tourists and loyal locals alike.

The 'yum cha' culture was very different," Chui tells us, referring to the days when the cozy tea house was still part of a seven-story public housing estate in Lok Fu. "The way people lived was completely different back then! We spread our tables and chairs all over the floor outside our shop. It used to be much louder and busier."

> "Our recipes have stayed the same throughout the years. Our customers' tastes have stayed the same as well."

"Making dim sum is such hard work," Chui says. "We don't get to rest during the day, making one basket of dim sum after another. When the lava custard buns run out, we have to make more."

"We decide what and how much dim sum to make depending on how many customers we have at a time. It's all quite ad hoc," Chui explains. "Take our fried milk custard, for example. We don't prepare it in advance. We calculate the number of customers and make an amount that's roughly enough for them so we can keep our dim sum hot and always freshly made."

Despite changing trends over the years, Sun Hing has never strayed from its original offerings. "Our recipes have stayed the same throughout the years. Our customers' tastes have stayed the same as well," Chui says. "There are only minor changes — we use less oil in our cooking now. Some traditional dim sum dishes are also gradually disappearing, such as glutinous rice rolls, quail eggs, and siu mai made with pork liver."

Customers at Sun Hing are not only there for the food. "Our long-time customers care a lot about their tea, which is as important as the dim sum to them," Chui says. "They like to wash their own teacups, because it's a ritual to them. They really enjoy the entire process of making and drinking tea. Also, anyone who loves tea knows a good cup of tea depends on the temperature, so they wash their own teacups with the hot water provided on the table in order to have better control of the temperature. [Making sure everything is clean] is another reason they wash the tableware before they eat and drink."

Chui Kwok-hing, owner of Sun Hing (新興食家 *sun1 hing1 sick6 gah1*)

203

GOING RETRO

Lin Heung Kui might have only opened in 2009, but it is part of a revered family franchise that has been making its mark since 1902, when it first debuted in Guangdong province. The multi-level Sai Ying Pun restaurant is one of the remaining venues to use dim sum trolleys to sell its steaming hot dim sum.

"Dim sum chefs usually do not make any dim sum dish on their own," chef Sze Wing-ching, who has been working with the Lin Heung brand for over 20 years, explains. "We have a chef in charge of pan-frying and deep-frying, a chef responsible for preparing the dim sum stuffing, one for preparing the bamboo steamer, another in charge of steaming, one in charge of the rice noodle rolls, and so on."

"For most of my time as a dim sum chef, I worked in the role of preparing the stuffing, including preparing the prawns inside the har gow and the meat inside of the siu mai," Sze says. "It's one of the most important positions in the kitchen. Making buns is another senior position. Only the senior chefs get to make har gow. You need experience to get the dumpling skins just right."

"Only the senior chefs get to make har gow. You need experience to get the dumpling skins just right."

Sze Wing-ching, chef at Lin Heung Kui (蓮香居 *leen4 hurng1 gui1*)

TEA TIME

The Fukien Tea Company is a retailer that has been supplying in-house-roasted tea leaves to consumers all over the world, for more than 60 years.

"My father opened this tea company in 1952," owner Patrick Yeung tells us. "In the beginning, we mostly exported tea leaves to other regions in South East Asia or Europe. There was not much business opportunity within the city for tea leaves then. Gradually, we set up shop and began doing retail as well."

"In Hong Kong, Pu'er, tieguanyin and shoumei are the most common styles of tea," Yeung says. "Pu'er started out as the common man's tea. People drank it as a sort of digestif, in huge portions. It was not a high-end tea. But about 20 years ago, in the 80s, the Taiwanese started turning Pu'er into one of the most expensive teas around. They started aging the Pu'er tea, and Pu'er tea that was 50 to 60 years old became a valuable commodity."

Yeung has also noticed another trend in recent years: the younger generation prefers to drink lighter, more floral teas like the six-hour-roast tieguanyin, instead of the traditional, much stronger

60-hour-roast. "It works better for me because I sell both types of tea at the same price," Yeung says, "and the light roast requires a lot less work."

There's a general etiquette to follow when making teas. "When making tea, pour the water into the teapot. The first pour is only for quickly rinsing the tea leaves," Yeung explains. "The leaves are usually handled by hand so it's good to give them a quick clean."

"Next, pour more hot water into the teapot and let the leaves steep," Yeung continues, "and also pour hot water over the teacups to keep them warm. Leave the tea to steep for about 6 to 10 seconds, and then pour it out. If you steep for too long, the tea will turn bitter despite its quality."

Patrick Yeung and son, owners of Fukien Tea Company (福建茶行 *fook1 geen3 chah4 hawng2*)

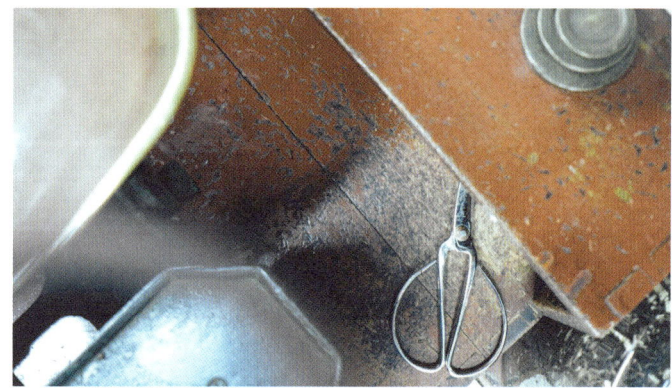

"In Hong Kong, Pu'er, tieguanyin and shoumei are the most common styles of tea."

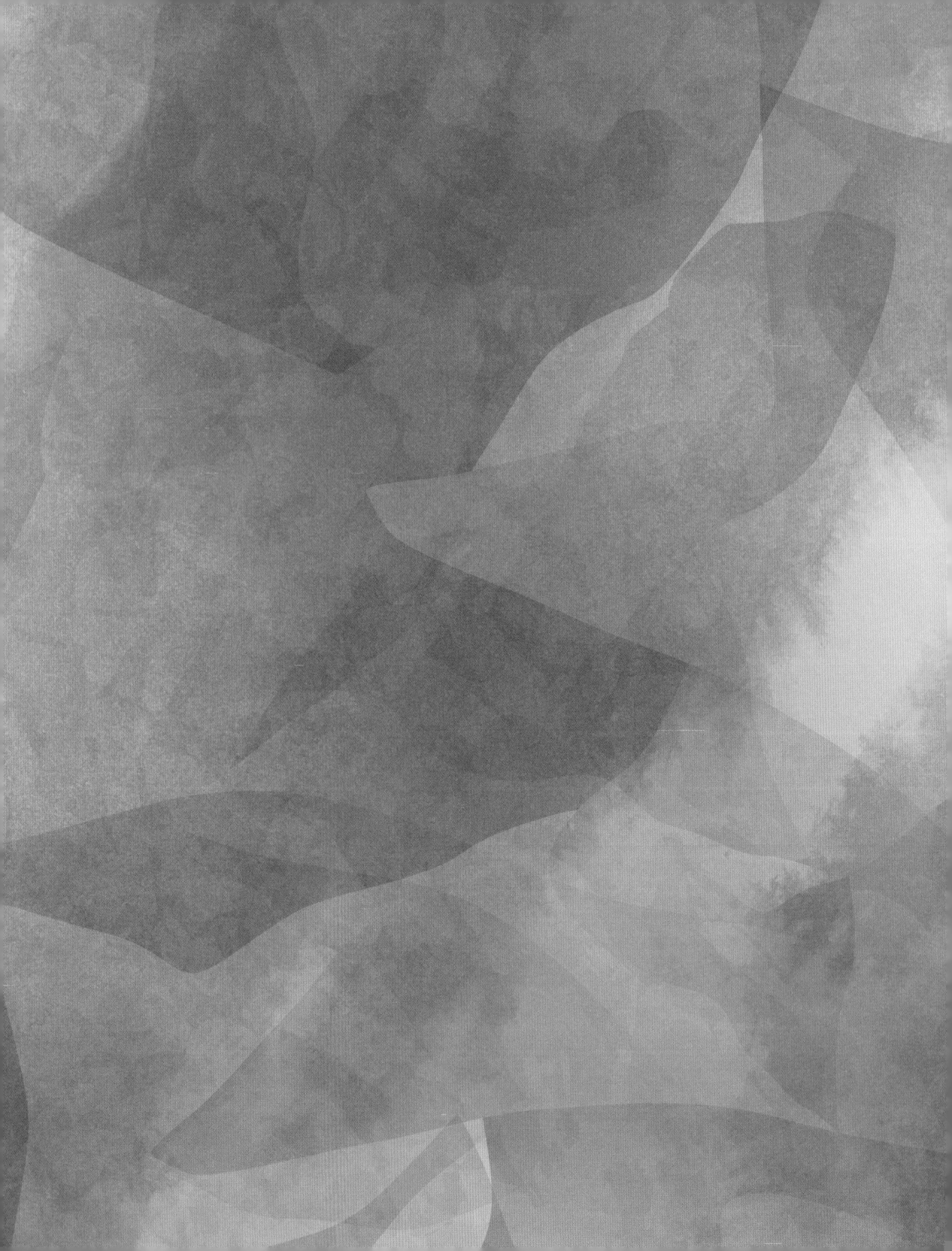

TRADITIONAL CHINESE MEDICINE

Food and medicine share the same roots, according to ancient Traditional Chinese Medicine wisdom. In Hong Kong, you can see this philosophy being applied to everything from herbal soups to everyday dishes.

It is impossible to talk about food culture in Hong Kong without also mentioning Traditional Chinese Medicine (TCM) at some point. In fact, TCM is a somewhat deceiving term because it has very little to do with how we define medicine in the western sense. It is, instead, an all-encompassing philosophy based on a converging set of Taoist, Confucianist and Buddhist theories and classification systems that extend into the realms of physical exercise as well as food consumption.

TCM originated in mainland China more than 2,000 years ago — built on a foundation of lyrically abstract hypotheses and empirical findings — and is widely practiced in Hong Kong today. Walk through any typical neighborhood, and you're bound to find a streetside Chinese pharmacy (中藥鋪 *johng1 yurk6 po2*) or dried goods shop (乾貨鋪 *gawn1 faw3 po2*) stocking hundreds of different herbs and remedies in glass jars and wooden cabinets. Local supermarkets usually dedicate a section or aisle to popular ingredients for making TCM soups.

But the truth is, you are inevitably dabbling in TCM just by being a human being with an appetite in Hong Kong — whether you realize it or not. The TCM motto is that you are exactly what you eat, and so by default, every edible thing would have a specific health-related function or consequence. Dried Job's tears barley might be a popular ingredient in TCM soups for its fever-reducing or "heat"-clearing properties (more on this later), but even tofu — which is cooked and consumed by local Hongkongers on a regular basis — has been attributed digestion-improving and joint-pain-relieving characteristics.

There are volumes and volumes of literature in the TCM world dedicated to categorizing the nature and functions of any and every ingredient known to mankind, such that the lines really start to blur between everyday food and official oral medicine. That's because from the TCM perspective, food can directly cause or prevent an illness, and by the same logic, it can also treat or exacerbate it.

TCM is a seductively holistic approach to things. We especially love this much-touted motto that sums up the importance of food for general health: "Food and Medicine Share the Same Roots" (藥食同源 *yurk6 sick6 tohng4 yune4*). As you can probably gather, TCM is a largely preemptive and proactive approach to well-being. The dietary branch of TCM advocates stopping an illness from developing via proper food consumption, rather than waiting to treat the illness using medication. And who doesn't like the sound of that?

Roughly speaking, TCM can be broken down into two integrated philosophies: Yin Yang (陰陽 *yum1 yurng4*), and Five Phases (五行 *mm5 hung6*).

YIN YANG
陰陽 *yum1 yurng4*

The Chinese Yin Yang theory is an extremely romantic one. It essentially states that for every thing, action, or concept, there exists a complementing opposite. And by extension: without one, there cannot be the other. For the concept of hot, there is the counter-concept of cold. For the female form, there is the contrasting male form. For the upward direction, there is the contrary downward direction. Balance is the modus operandi for the Yin Yang pairs: too much or too little of one or the other will disrupt the natural order of things. TCM applies Yin Yang theory by stressing that one should always strive for balance in diet.

To understand how to maintain this balance, the human body can be viewed in Yin Yang terms — Yin being associated with vaguely feminine properties, and Yang with more masculine ones. Someone who's prone to chills and cold limbs is said to have a cold Yin body composition (體質 *tai2 jutt1*). Someone who sweats a lot is likely to have a hot Yang build. A super-energetic, overly hyper person would err on the strong Yang side of the spectrum, while an easily fatigued individual would fall on the weak Yin side. Someone with a heavy frame or oily skin would be damp Yin, while someone with a light frame or dry skin would be dry Yang. If you have too much Yin in your body, you would need to intake less Yin-nature foods or balance things out with more Yang-nature foods — and vice versa.

This notion of balance extends to external circumstances. During the hot summer months, one is advised to consume more inherently "cooling" (涼 *lurng4*) Yin foods to counteract the heat. In the same vein, one will hear the term "hot air" (熱氣 *yeet6 hay3*) used to describe the Yang foods that tend to heat up the body. When one feels cold or low in energy, one can ingest these high-energy Yang foods to help the body stay warm.

At the same time, it is possible to ingest too much Yin- or Yang-natured foods, which can cause damage to the body. For instance, over-consumption of salty Yin-natured foods is supposed to cause damage to the bones, as well as increase one's chances of developing wrinkles. The key is to ingest everything in moderation.

Keep in mind though that TCM dictates almost everything in the abstract sense, so the concepts of hot Yang and cold Yin food don't necessarily relate to the food's physical temperature. Every food source is assigned innate "heating" or "cooling" properties based on historical observation and theory. And that's just the beginning.

YIN FOODS VS. YANG FOODS: AN OVERVIEW

Throughout our research, we've encountered conflicting explanations of the nature of yin and yang foods. Because Yin Yang theory itself is so abstract and broad, there are bound to be many different interpretations. It's also good to remember that Yin and Yang are not absolute concepts, and everything is relative. Generally speaking, the Yin Yang food spectrum can be summed up in the chart below:

Yin Foods	Neutral	Yang Foods
Feminine	–	Masculine
Sour / Bitter / Salty	–	Spicy / Sweet / Bland
Cool / Cold / Cooling (涼 lurng4)	No Temperature Interference	Warm / Hot / Warming (熱 yeet6)
Downward	–	Upward
Cultivated and eaten in spring / summer; avoided during winter	Can be eaten year-round	Cultivated and eaten in autumn / winter; avoided during summer
Energy-restraining	–	Energy-promoting
Damp (濕 sup1)	–	Dry (燥 cho3)
Eaten raw or steamed; low-calorie	–	Cooked in high heat; high-calorie
Green and white foods	–	Red and orange foods
Green vegetables, fruits, seafood	Rice, carrots, corn, soybeans, sugar	Dairy products, red meat, poultry, spices
Treats "hot" diseases (i.e. rashes, heartburn)	–	Treats "cold" diseases (i.e. anemia, chills)

FIVE PHASES
五行 *mm5 hung6*

Five is a ubiquitous number in traditional Chinese philosophy, and you can really see its application in TCM theory. There are five major (and six minor) "organ" systems (臟腑 *jawng6 fu2*) in the human body. There are five official tastes (五味 *mm5 may6*) perceived by the human tongue (not including bland, which is recognized as a taste but has no place in the pentalogy). There are five different colors that all foods can be categorized into — based essentially on their actual physical color. And these five-isms all miraculously correspond to the five distinct natural "phases" (五行 *mm5 hung4*) of Wood, Fire, Earth, Metal, and Water, which in turn dictates the particular nature, or TCM property, of a food.

Again, everything here is meant in the abstract sense: for instance, the "liver" label doesn't necessarily correspond to the actual liver organ, although it does encompass parts of its functions, plus a whole lot more. Our advice is to not get too caught up with all the definitions and to just go with the flow. When applied with common sense and a healthy dose of skepticism, TCM can add an interesting layer of analysis to one's dietary lifestyle.

Wood 木 *mook6*	Fire 火 *faw2*	Earth 土 *toh2*	Metal 金 *gum1*	Water 水 *sui2*
Helps "liver" dispel toxins	Improves circulation	Helps digestion	Keeps skin moist and nourished	Strengthens "kidney"
Sour (酸 *sune1*)	Bitter (苦 *foo2*)	Sweet (甜 *teem4*)	Pungent / Spicy (辛辣 *sun1 laht6*)	Salty (鹹 *hahm4*)
Helps stop thirst; controls urination	Clears "heat" in the body; helps with skin issues	Boosts energy; increases appetite	Promotes blood circulation; increases appetite	Prevents constipation; relieves swelling
Airy	Hot	Damp	Dry	Cold
Spring	Summer	Last two weeks per season	Autumn	Winter
Liver (肝 *gawn1*)	Heart (心 *sum1*)	Spleen (脾 *pay4*)	Lung (肺 *fai3*)	Kidney (腎 *sun6*)
Blood storage; digestion control; related to gall bladder (膽 *dahm2*) system	Blood circulation; related to small intestine (小腸 *siu2 churng2*) system	Muscle and limb control; related to stomach (胃 *wai6*) system	Fluid control; related to large intestine (大腸 *dye6 churng2*) system	Fundamental organ; bone development; related to bladder (膀胱 *pawng4 gwawng1*) system
New Yang	Full Yang	Balanced	New Yin	Full Yin
Preserved plums, vinegar	Lotus seed, beer, coffee	Ginseng, dried longan, red date	Ginger, garlic, scallion, wasabi	Sea cucumber, sea urchin, shrimp
Green foods	Red foods	Yellow foods	White foods	Black foods

FIVE PHASES AND THEIR ASSOCIATIONS

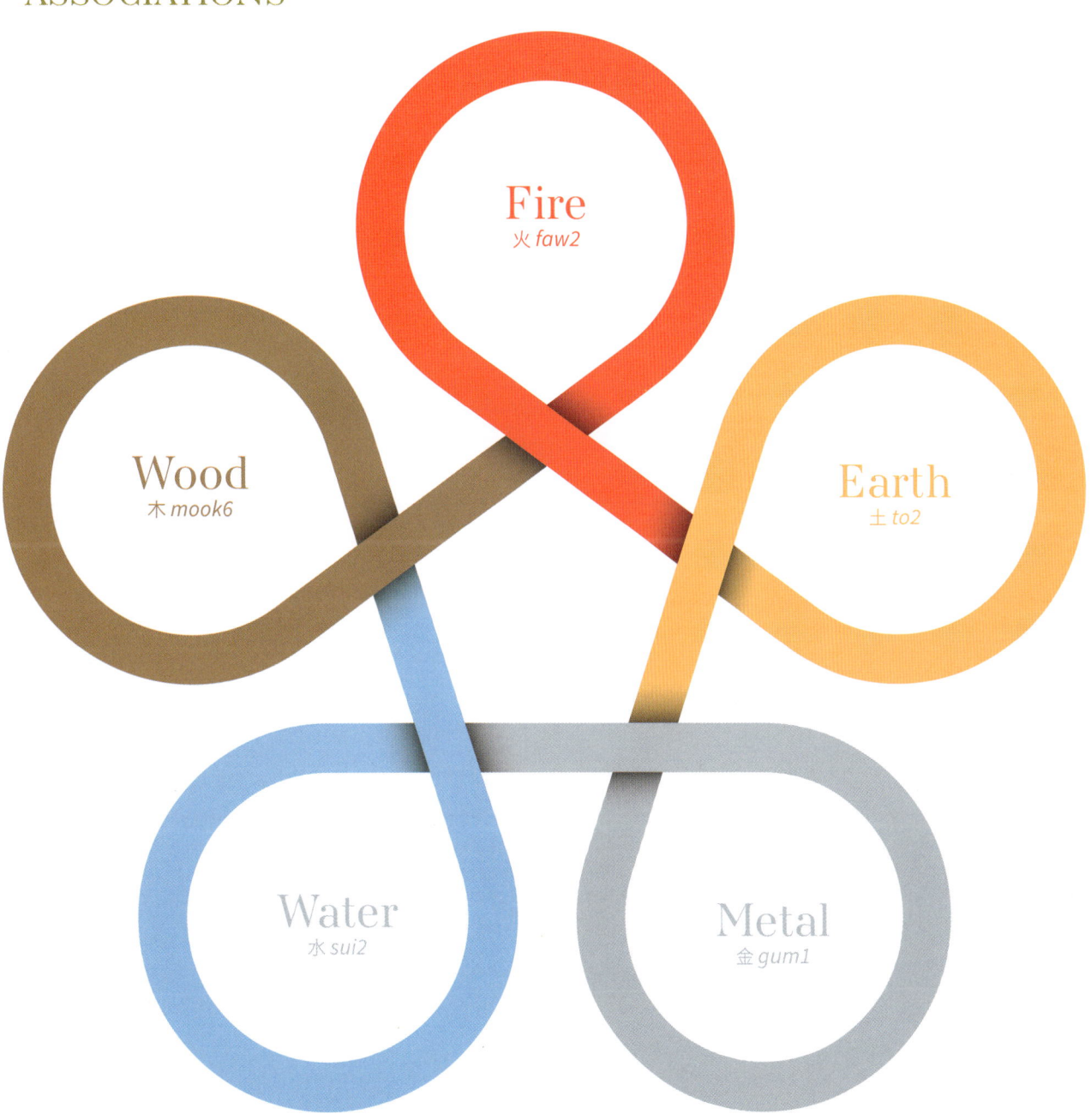

COMMON HONG KONG FOODS AND THEIR TCM PROPERTIES

Here is a sample list of foods, along with their place in the TCM spectrum. Please treat this as a reference only and use your own discretion and judgment when it comes to healthy eating.

PORK
豬肉 *ju1 yook6*

WARM | SALTY

Helps loosen the bowels; nourishes the blood

SCALLION
蔥 *chohng1*

WARM | PUNGENT (SPICY)

Helps with flu and cold symptoms; opens up skin's pores

PEANUT
花生 *fah1 sung1*

NEUTRAL | SWEET, BITTER

Helps with dry cough, constipation

LEMON
檸檬 *ning4 mohng1*

COOL | SOUR, SWEET

Helps with constipation, dry coughs, swelling

WATERMELON
西瓜 *sai1 gwah1*

COOL | SWEET

Rehydrates, cools the body

QI, BLOOD, FLUIDS AND MORE

In TCM, there are numerous references to "Qi" (氣 *hay3*) — literally, "air" in Chinese — which is pretty much a catch-all term that can be interpreted as one's vital energy, life essence, or life source. Qi can also be loosely associated with one's breath, or the flow of the breath through one's body. (Remember: don't stress about the definitions and just go with the flow — pun intended.) One can be deficient in Qi, and the Qi can stagnate, "sink" or be rebellious (moving in all sorts of directions). Some of the same patterns that manifest in Qi can also be applied to the blood and fluids circulating within the body. Naturally, there are types of foods that can be taken to help lift (upward), lower (downward), float (outward) or sink (inward) said Qi, blood, and fluids back to balance.

To determine one's diagnosis, TCM doctors would typically conduct a checkup by "reading" one's body for physical clues; listening to one's voice and breathing; asking questions to assess one's general health; and finally, checking one's pulse. The doctor would assess the amount of "spirit" (神 *sun4*) one possesses, and other telltale signs like one's body shape and the color of one's face and tongue. It would take a whole other book to describe the art of TCM diagnosis. But the key takeaway is this: whatever conclusions a TCM doctor makes regarding one's health, a set of foods or herbal remedies along with perhaps some acupuncture or other Chinese physical therapy would be recommended to set one back to balance.

HERBAL TEAS
涼茶 *lurng4 chah4*

Streetside herbal tea shops (涼茶鋪 *lurng4 chah4 po2*) selling dark-colored brews in pre-poured bowls and cups are many Hongkongers' first point of access to specialized TCM remedies.

The herbal teas are also known as cooling teas (涼茶 *lurng4 chah4*) for their inherently body-cooling properties — although they are typically served hot or lukewarm in temperature.

Although not a specifically Cantonese concept, herbal tea shops are much more popular in southern China due to the region's hotter and more humid weather.

Different herbal teas serve different functions. The 24-herbs tea (廿四味 *yah6 say3 may2*) is a typical concoction found at the shops. The recipe varies from shop to shop but could include ingredients like chrysanthemum flower (菊花 *gook1 fah1*), luo han guo (羅漢果 *law4 hawn3 gwaw2*), bamboo leaf (竹葉 *jook1 yeep6*), and mulberry leaf (桑葉 *sawng1 yeep6*). The extremely bitter tea is supposed to relieve sore throats, inflammation, and help with common cold and flu symptoms.

There's also the five-flower tea (五花茶 *mm5 fah1 chah4*), which can be made from bombax (木棉花 *mook6 meen4 fah1*), chrysanthemum flower, honeysuckle (銀花 *un2 fah1*), frangipani (雞蛋花 *gai1 dahn2 fah1*) and kudzu vine (葛花 *gawt3 fah1*) — although the recipe can differ from shop to shop. This tea is supposed to help with fatigue and indigestion and can also act as a diuretic.

RECOMMENDED SOUPS FOR EACH SEASON

SPRING
JOB'S TEARS PEARL BARLEY SOUP
薏米水
yee3 mai5 sui2

SUMMER
WINTER MELON SOUP
冬瓜湯
dohng1 gwah1 tawng1

AUTUMN
SNOW PEAR SOUP
雪耳雪梨糖水
sute3 yee3 sute3 lay4 tawng4 sui2

WINTER
PORK STOMACH AND PEPPER SOUP
胡椒豬肚湯
woo4 jiu1 ju1 toh5 tawng1

A HEALTHY PRACTICE

Dr. Gladys Leung is a private TCM practitioner as well as health consultant in Hong Kong. She goes by the Chinese saying, "If there's blockage, there's pain," (不通則痛 *butt1 tohng1 jutt1 tohng3*) referring to the theory that one's fluids, qi, and blood must all flow smoothly for one's body to remain healthy.

Leung advocates a balanced diet that includes meat to maintain a healthy body. "We're animals," she says. "We have blood and flesh. So we should eat things that have blood and flesh for nourishment."

"Chinese food therapy has a very interesting concept: every type of food enters a certain organ meridian (臟腑經絡 *jawng6 fu2 ging1 lawk3*)," Leung explains. "For example, the chrysanthemum flower enters the liver and can be used to treat 'liver fire' (肝火 *gawn1 faw2*). Liver fire will lead to red eyes, since the liver is related to and affects our eyes. If you feel hot or your eyes are dry and red, you can boil some chrysanthemum with water to drink."

She also believes that western medicine and TCM can be used in collaboration with each other. "I feel we should incorporate TCM and western medicine together. The best is to have western medicine's lab reports and blood tests to support our diagnoses. That would be perfect."

Dr. Gladys Leung, founder of TCM with Dr. Gladys Leung (德馨堂 *duck1 hing1 tawng4*)

"If there's blockage, there's pain."

AN HERBAL REMEDY

Elaine and Martin Lam are the third-generation proprietors of Good Spring Company, an herbal tea shop and TCM clinic on Cochrane Street in Central. My great-grandfather sold Chinese herbs on the street," says Martin Lam. "Sometimes he would use the herbs to make teas and sell them. My grandfather learned from him and opened a shop in Hong Kong to sell herbal teas. We later also started selling Chinese herbs and having in-house doctors."

"Herbal tea is very representative of Chinese culture," Lam continues. "When you have herbal tea, you only taste the sweetness after the bitterness. It's very traditional Chinese thinking. You have to learn, work hard and gather knowledge before you can succeed."

One of the shop's top-selling products is the turtle jelly (龜苓膏 *gwai1 ling4 go1*), made from ground turtle shell and ingredients like spreading hedyotis herb (蛇舌草 *seh4 seet3 cho2*), Chinese

"When you have herbal tea, you only taste the sweetness after the bitterness. It's a very traditional Chinese thinking."

prayer bead grass (雞骨草 *gai1 gwutt1 cho2*), and dendrobium orchid (石斛 *seck6 hook6*).

"Turtle jelly can 'clear heat' (清熱 *ching1 yeet6*) and 'moisturize' your intestines (潤腸 *yuhn6 churng4*)," Elaine Lam explains. "The turtle shell and dendrobium nourish your Yin (滋陰 *jee1 yum1*). You can eat it hot or cold. If your digestive system is not as good, it's better to eat it warm."

The streetside shop also offers freshly made herbal teas for a drink-and-go experience, including a variation of the five-flower tea and the popular 24-herbs. "I drink 24-herbs every day," Martin Lam says. "It helps with digestion (消滯 *siu1 jai6*) and cleanses your stomach and intestines (清腸 *ching1 churng4*) if you eat too much hot food. Don't look at it as an herbal tea, but as a tea that helps with digestion."

Elaine and Martin Lam, owners of Good Spring Company (春回堂藥行 *chuhn1 wooi4 tawng4 yurk6 hawng2*)

PRUNELLA HERBAL TEA

夏枯草
hah6 foo1 cho2

🕐 1 hr   🎣 1 night   🥣 6 bowls

This simple formula is great for those who do not get enough sleep, as well as for countering coughs, sore throats and the side effects of alcohol consumption. Prunella is said to have great heat-clearing properties. Luo han guo is supposed to be very effective for soothing a cough, sore throat, or bad breath. Thunberg fritillary is optional, but under TCM theory works wonders in calming down a painful sore throat. The soybeans are meant to be a neutral ingredient that adds sweetness to the tea.

INGREDIENTS

1 catty (600g) prunella   夏枯草 *hah6 foo1 cho2*
50g soybeans   黃豆 *wawng4 dau2*
1 piece luo han guo   羅漢果 *law4 hawn3 gwaw2*
50g thunberg fritillary   浙貝母 *jeet3 booi3 mo5*

METHOD

1. Soak soybeans in tap water, and let sit for at least 8 hours.

2. Rinse all ingredients in running water, and soak in water briefly. Break luo han guo into large pieces.

3. Put all ingredients into a large pot. Add enough water to get it 2 to 3 inches above the herbs. Boil for about 1 hour.

HERBS, SPICES, PRESERVED GOODS

Spices and herbs are an intricate part of Cantonese cuisine. The diverse and exotic ingredients that belong to this loosely defined category are used to enhance flavors and to impart character into specific Chinese dishes — and they are also an integral part of Traditional Chinese Medicine (TCM).

To avoid confusion, we want to clarify that the term "herb" in this chapter refers to the dried plant as well as animal parts that are used mainly for Cantonese medicinal — and by default, culinary — purposes. This is much broader than the popular conventional definition, which refers only to the leafy or herbaceous plants that are used for regular food preparation. The term "spice" generally refers to plant parts that are not leafy in nature, like seeds, bark, root or fruit. But as far as we know, there is no worldwide standard in terms of classification — so if we could have it our way, we would just call them all Chinese herbspices!

Many of the ingredients can be found at TCM pharmacies (中藥鋪 *johng1 yurk6 po2*), dried goods stores (乾貨鋪 *gawn1 faw3 po2*), some dried seafood shops (海味鋪 *hoy2 may2 po2*), supermarkets (超級市場 *chiu1 kup1 see5 churng4*), and niche stalls at indoor and outdoor wet markets (街市 *gye1 see5*).

Most of the herbs and spices are sold dried, which makes for relatively easy storage in a humid city like Hong Kong. You'll find the raw ingredients laid out in barrels and containers at street-level TCM shops, or sold in branded packages at the more conventional retailers. Nowadays, you will find shops that stock herbs and spices as well as a whole range of other general dried goods like seafood, dried pickled vegetables, and ham.

To list all the seeds, leaves, roots, and other plant and animal parts that feature in Cantonese cooking would take an entire book on its own, but here are some common and popular ingredients that should serve as a solid introduction.

HERBS

Herbs will be defined here as both dried plant and animal parts used in cooking and medicine.

❶ JOB'S TEARS / CHINESE PEARL BARLEY
薏仁 *yee3 yun4*

Job's tears are also known as coixseeds or Chinese pearl barley, and feature frequently in Cantonese dessert soups as well as health drinks — in other words, soaked in liquid of some form. In TCM, the mild-flavored Job's Tears function as a diuretic.

❷ MUNG BEAN
綠豆 *look6 dau2*

Just like the red bean, the mung bean, known colloquially as "green bean" in Cantonese, is the star ingredient in a popular dessert soup known as mung bean stew (綠豆沙 *look6 dau2 sah1*). The beans can also be turned into puddings (綠豆糕 *look6 dau2 go1*) and added to savory soups. In TCM wisdom, the mung bean helps cool down the body.

❸ WOLFBERRIES / GOJI BERRIES
杞子 *gay2 jee2*

The brightly colored and mildly flavored wolfberries feature in many Cantonese soups, dessert soups, and teas. It is a highly regarded ingredient in TCM, and the sweet fruit is said to help with insomnia.

❹ LILY PETALS
百合 *bahk3 hup6*

Lily petals are another common element in savory meat-based soups as well as dessert soups. From the TCM perspective, the flowers are supposed to help calm the nerves.

❺ JUJUBES
紅棗 *hohng4 jo2*

Jujubes, also known as Chinese red dates, feature frequently in Cantonese soups and desserts. The fruit turns to an intense shade of red once dried, and has a meaty, plummy taste. In TCM terms, the jujube meat is said to help calm the mind.

❻ APRICOT KERNELS
南北杏 *nahm4 buck1 hung6*

Apricot kernels, found within the pits of the fruit, are often mistakenly called almonds in English. Sliced apricot kernels are added to savory pork-based soups, and in TCM they are supposed to treat coughs. There are two styles of kernels: the bitter north (北 *buck1*) kernel, and the sweeter south (南 *nahm4*) kernel.

⑦ CHINESE YAM
淮山 *wye4 sahn1*

Dried Chinese yam slices, which are hard and brittle compared to their fresh counterparts, are yet another popular ingredient in savory chicken-based soups and soup desserts. The health benefits of Chinese yam, in TCM terms, include strengthening the immune system and improving digestion.

⑧ GINSENG
人参 *yun4 sum1*

The sweet and bitter ginseng plant root is treated as a luxury product and its value is reflected in its hefty prices. In Hong Kong, ginseng is usually sold dried, and it may be brewed as a tea or added to soups. There are many varieties of ginseng available, although nowadays the North American white ginseng (花旗参 *fah1 kay4 sum1*) is one of the most sought-after. In TCM terms, ginseng is said to help improve memory and reduce fatigue.

⑨ DEER VELVET ANTLER
鹿茸 *look6 yohng4*

Deer velvet antler slices are used in various TCM tonic soups, and depending on the part of the antler used, can supposedly help with everything from general growth to arthritic pain. Appearance-wise, they are hard, triangular wood-like pieces with a fuzzy coating.

⑩ GINKGO NUT
銀杏 *un4 hung6*

The ginkgo nut is an optional ingredient in savory, pork-based soups. The nuts are sold either in their shells or fully peeled, but are used in their peeled form in Cantonese cooking. In TCM terms, the sweet and bitter ginkgo is said to help those with asthmatic symptoms like shortness of breath.

CHINESE RED BEAN (ADZUKI)
紅豆 *hohng4 dau2*

The adzuki bean, literally "red bean" in Cantonese, is so common that it has pretty much fully blurred the line between functional "herb" and mainstream ingredient. The bean can be turned into stews (紅豆沙 *hohng4 dau2 sah1*), puddings (紅豆糕 *hohng4 dau2 go1*), and even iced drinks (紅豆冰 *hohng4 dau2 bing1*). In paste form (豆沙 *dau6 sah1*), it can be used as filling for steamed buns (豆沙包 *dau6 sah1 bao1*). Adzuki beans are said to help with symptoms like swelling and bloating.

TURTLE SHELL POWDER
龜板 *gwai1 bahn2*

Turtle shell powder, ground from the plastron — or bottom shell — of a turtle, is best known as the key ingredient in turtle jelly (龜苓膏 *gwai1 ling4 go1*), a black jelly pudding sold at herbal tea shops across the city. According to TCM, turtle shell helps one develop good skin and a smooth complexion. Some shops these days sell turtle jelly without actually using turtle shell powder, but substitutes that boast the same effects.

CORDYCEPS FLOWER
蟲草花 *chohng4 cho2 fah1*

The caterpillar fungus (冬蟲夏草 *dohng1 chohng4 hah6 cho2*) — sometimes called cordyceps — has a slightly more romantic name in Cantonese that translates to "Winter Worm Summer Grass". Essentially, this parasitic fungus feeds and lives off of underground moth larvae, eventually killing its host and growing its own fungal body as an extension to the mummified larva carcass. Although not a common ingredient in Cantonese cooking, the caterpillar fungus does have its place in TCM literature, with purported aphrodisiac powers and hefty prices to match. The more affordable cordyceps flower, on the other hand, has become an increasingly popular ingredient in Cantonese cooking, making appearances in homes and fancy Cantonese restaurants alike. The cordyceps flower is technically the artificially cultivated fungus, or mushroom, part of the caterpillar fungus.

SPICES

Spices might not feature as prominently in Hong Kong-style cooking as it does in other Chinese regions, but Hongkongers do know how to use a variety of spices to flavor and enhance their dishes.

❶ WHITE PEPPER
白胡椒 *bahk6 woo4 jiu1*

Ground white pepper is a common tabletop seasoning found at local Hong Kong restaurants, especially those that serve congee and soup noodles. White pepper — essentially, the seeds of the dried peppercorn plant with the outer layer removed — has a more delicate yet very distinct aroma compared to the black peppercorn.

❷ STAR ANISE
八角 *baht3 gawk3*

Star anise is a common spice around the world, and it can also be found in many intensely flavored Cantonese recipes. Whether used as a whole spice in marinades and Chiu Chow-style sauces (鹵水汁 *lo5 sui2 jup1*), or ground to a powder in a five-spice mix, the star anise is a handy ingredient to keep in the kitchen.

❸ CASSIA
肉桂 *yook6 gwai3*

Cassia is an extremely aromatic variety of cinnamon. In ground form, it makes up one of the components of five-spice powder. In bark form (桂皮 *gwai3 pay4*), it is used in soy sauce-based marinades and Chiu Chow-style sauces.

❹ GINGER ROOT
薑 *gurng1*

The pungent ginger root is a very important spice in Cantonese cuisine. It adds a punch to cooked savory dishes, and spices up dessert soups. It is used in fresh, dried and powdered form.

SAND GINGER
沙薑 *sah1 gurng1*

The powdered form of sand ginger, a subtype of the galangal, can be found in modest doses in Cantonese roast and steamed poultry recipes. The highly aromatic spice has a sweet peppery nose. The plant itself belongs to the ginger family, although its flavor profile is milder and less spicy than the more common ginger root.

DRIED TANGERINE PEEL
果皮 / 陳皮 gwaw2 pay4 / chun4 pay4

Dried tangerine peel adds a tangy, plummy kick to Cantonese dessert soups, and sometimes to a savory dish like steamed fish, or to steamed beef balls (牛肉球 au4 yook6 kau4) found in dim sum halls. In TCM terms, the tangerine peel is said to stimulate the appetite. Sugar-dusted dried tangerine peel (九製陳皮 gau2 jai3 chun4 pay4), eaten on its own as a snack, can also be found at local confectioneries and supermarkets.

FIVE-SPICE POWDER
五香粉 mm5 hurng1 fun2

Five-spice powder is a common ingredient in Cantonese roast recipes and marinades. Recipes vary but the powder can contain everything from ground fennel seeds (小茴香籽 siu2 wooi4 hurng1 jee2), star anise, cloves (丁香 ding1 hurng1), cassia bark, ginger root and dried tangerine peel to Sichuan peppercorn (花椒 fah1 jiu1). From seasoning roast duck (燒鴨 siu1 ahp3) to barbecued pork (叉燒 chah1 siu1), the powder gives foods an extra level of fragrance and flavor. It is also a common soup flavor for noodles served at local diners.

DRIED AND PRESERVED GOODS

Besides dried herbs and spices, Hongkongers also love to cook with, and eat, dried and preserved goods of all kinds. Just walk through any typical wet market in the city and you'll be able to find everything from pickled vegetables to shriveled-up sea creatures to preserved eggs.

DRIED SEAFOOD
海味 *hoy2 may2*

Dried seafood (海味 *hoy2 may2*) — literally meaning "flavors of the ocean" — is an extremely lucrative trade in Hong Kong. This is no coincidence, since Cantonese cuisine does tend to have a strong focus on marine-based goods, fresh or otherwise.

There are streets that are dedicated to dried seafood in the Sheung Wan and Sai Ying Pun districts, known collectively as Seafood Street. Many of these streetside shops act as distributors as well as retailers, and rather than specializing in one particular product, they tend to carry a little bit of everything to attract as many customers as possible.

A lot of the dried seafood is considered edible luxury. There's the cartilaginous ❶ fish maw (花膠 *fah1 gao1*), or the swim bladder of the fish, which the Cantonese love to use in savory soups. There's the ❷ sea cucumber (海參 *hoy2 sum1*): a sausage-like sea-floor creature that turns into a jelly-like blob when cooked. There's the shark's fin (魚翅 *yu4 chee3*), which is served at Chinese banquets or fancy dinners in a famous stew of the same name — although the dish is getting rarer and rarer these days, given concerns about the alleged cruel treatment of sharks that are harvested only for their fins. There's the ❸ conpoy (乾瑤柱 *gawn1 yiu4 chu5*), a form of dried scallop that features in Cantonese XO sauce, and is a natural "umami" agent in numerous savory dishes. Then there's the ❹ abalone (鮑魚 *bao1 yu4*), king of them all. The wrinkly creature features on fancy banquet menus and is usually Chinese-style-braised in an intense and viscous sauce or broth. Its shape resembles ancient Chinese gold ingots, giving it an extra auspicious quality (see Local Restaurants chapter).

The once-common but now increasingly rare salted fish (鹹魚 *hahm4 yu2*), sold whole, is typically served chopped-up as a topping to rice and stir-fries. It can be made from different varieties of fish, including blue threadfin (馬友 *ma5 yau5*). The ❺ dried oyster (蠔豉 *ho4 see2*) can be added to soups and congee. Then there are the ❻ tiny dried fish / whitebait (銀魚乾 *un4 yu4 gawn1*) and ❼ dried shrimp (蝦米 *hah1 mai5*) that can be used as a topping to congee and stir-fries.

As a general rule, the dried seafood needs to first be rehydrated by soaking in a bowl of lukewarm water before cooking.

CURED MEAT
臘肉 *lahp6 yook6*

There are many varieties of cured meats eaten in China, but the Cantonese in particular are known for their ⑥ preserved pork sausages (臘腸 *lahp6 churng2*), usually sold by the pair and hung on strings. The sausages are available in different meat-to-fat ratios, with the lean ones being generally more expensive. Sausages made from duck liver (潤腸 *yuhn2 churng2*) and pig's blood (血腸 *hute3 churng2*) are also consumed.

Another popular pork product — though not exactly from Hong Kong or Guangdong Province — is the ⑦ Jinhua ham (金華火腿 *gum1 wah4 faw2 tui2*), from Jinhua city in Zhejiang Province. You'll see wrinkly yellowish hind legs hanging by the dozen in specialty shops. Underneath the waxy skin is a layer of pink, dense and extremely salty meat, sold by the chunk. The ham is typically served shredded: immersed in soups or used to flavor vegetable dishes.

The preserved whole duck (臘鴨 *lahp6 ahp3*) is another salt-cured specialty, sold pressed flat as a pancake. The duck is meant to be eaten steamed, with a bit of rice.

PRESERVED EGGS
醃蛋 *yeep3 dahn2*

There are eggs, and then there are preserved eggs. The ⑧ century egg (皮蛋 *pay4 dahn2*), sold at wet markets and some supermarkets, is a chicken or duck egg preserved in an alkaline solution made of calcium hydroxide (pickling lime), sodium carbonate (soda ash), and brine. Historically, the egg was caked in a solid clay and quicklime mixture. The century egg doesn't need to be cooked, and can be served in halves or quarters as an appetizer, or in chopped-up bits as a condiment to congee and vegetable dishes.

Another type is the ⑨ salted duck egg (鹹蛋 *hahm4 dahn2*), which is exactly as it sounds. The salt-cured eggs, when cooked, can be used to flavor congee and soups as well as to enhance savory dishes.

DRIED FUNGI
乾菌 *gawn1 kwun2*

Different varieties of mushrooms and fungi are used extensively in Cantonese cooking. The ⑩ shiitake mushroom (香菇 *hurng1 goo1*) and its most highly prized variety, the donko shiitake (冬菇 *dohng1 goo1*) (literally, "winter mushroom") are used in soups, stir-fries, braised dishes and Buddhist vegetarian dishes alike.

Floppy, gelatinous tree fungi like the thick, black wood ear (木耳 *mook6 yee5*); the thinner, black and slightly more translucent cloud ear (雲耳 *wun4 yee5*); and the white snow ear (雪耳 *sute3 yee5*) (also known as silver ear) can be used in savory soups, dessert soups, and stir-fries. Although sold dried, the fungi need to be rehydrated by soaking in a bowl of lukewarm water for at least half an hour before cooking.

PICKLED VEGETABLES
醃菜 *yeep3 choy3*

Pickled Chinese vegetables — preserved with salt, brine or sugar — are mostly sold "dried" (as in, not suspended in liquid like western-style pickles), and feature prominently at dried goods stalls. They are used to season congee and soups, enhance meat dishes, and depending on the variety, are sometimes eaten on their own as an appetizer. The different types available represent different regional preservation styles in China, although melting pot Hong Kong has adopted many of them as its own. There are the ⑪ salty or sweet mustard greens (梅菜 *mooi4 choy3*); the tart and salty ⑫ Chinese cabbage (咸酸菜 *hahm4 sune1 choy3*); the kimchi-like ⑬ mustard greens (榨菜 *jah3 choy3*); the super-savory ⑭ preserved daikon radish (菜脯 *choy3 po2*) and the savory ⑮ Chinese cabbage (雪菜 *sute3 choy3*).

OTHERS

The list of dried and preserved goods eaten by Hongkongers is virtually endless. Besides everything mentioned beforehand, plenty more miscellaneous items can be found at the wet market stalls and small goods shops around the city. There's dried bean curd (腐皮 *foo2 pay4*), which can be sold in ⑯ sheets (腐竹 *foo2 jook1*), ⑰ sticks (支竹 *jee1 jook1*), and ⑱ blocks (豆干 *dau6 gawn1*). There's dried snakeskin (乾蛇皮 *gawn1 seh4 pay4*), used in Cantonese tonic soups especially in the winter months, as TCM postulates that it is a "warming" agent. There is ⑲ fat choy (髮菜 *faht3 choy3*), a moss-like bacteria that resembles human hair and is a popular ingredient during Chinese New Year (see Food for Every Occasion chapter).

Then there's the ultra-luxurious bird's nest (燕窩 *yeen3 waw1*), made from the homes of swallows, and typically featured in dessert soups. Bird's nest, from the TCM point of view, is supposed to be full of health benefits like keeping your skin silky smooth.

AN AGE-OLD CURE

Leung Kwan is the proprietor of Man Lee Lung, a Chinese sausage and cured meat store on Des Voeux Road West.

"We make Guangdong-style sausages," Leung says, "but there are many other varieties from other provinces — such as Sichuan spicy sausages. Shanghai used to be known for its sweet sausages. Guangdong-style sausages respect more of the meat's original flavors and use relatively fewer spices and seasoning."

"Preserved sausages are uncooked. You cannot eat them raw," Leung explains. "One time a foreigner bought a preserved sausage and just tried to eat it on the spot. I immediately stopped him. You probably won't die from eating them raw, but it's not the way they're supposed to be eaten."

"Eating preserved sausages is simple enough for all of us, but making them is an art in itself."

Leung Kwan, owner of Man Lee Lung (萬利隆臘味家 *mahn6 lay6 lohng4 lahp6 may2 gah1*)

As to the best way to prepare Chinese sausages: "The best way to cook sausages is the simplest way — just steam and eat with rice," Leung says.

Sausage-making used to be an intensive process. "In the past, we began making sausages at 5:30am in the morning," Leung recalls. "After getting the ingredients ready, we would begin cutting up the pork meat. First, we would wash the meat in hot water, or else it would get too oily. Then we would rinse it one last time with cold water."

"We'd then wrap a sausage coating around a funnel, and use our fingers to push the meat mixture through. The meat mixture is prepared beforehand, by blending the exact proportion of fatty and lean meat together with sugar and rose wine."

But that wasn't the end. "We would then lay out all the sausages and puncture them with little holes. There would be a lot of oil and water in the sausages, so we'd need to get the moisture out. Then, we'd wash the sausages several times to clean the surface, and dry them under the sun for several hours. We would then dry them using charcoal — nowadays we use electricity."

Leung sums up the experience: "Eating preserved sausages is simple enough for all of us, but making them is an art in itself."

A TASTE OF LUXURY

One of the oldest shops on Seafood Street is Tung Hing Tai Kee on Des Voeux Road West, owned by Leung Wing-chiu. "Our shop has been open for 95 years. I'm a third-generation owner," says Leung.

Tung Hing Tai Kee boasts some of the most prestigious dried Cantonese ingredients in its inventory. "Our most expensive item is the caterpillar fungus from Tibet. We have some that are hundreds of thousands of dollars per catty. The dried fish maw of the Chinese bahaba fish is also hundreds of thousands of dollars a catty. It used to be even more expensive."

"Our most expensive item is the caterpillar fungus from Tibet."

Leung Wing-chiu, owner of Tung Hing Tai Kee (同興泰記 *tohng4 hing1 tye3 gay3*)

A FISHY TALE

Salted fish might have been commonplace in Hong Kong once upon a time, but these days the delicacy is getting rarer and rarer. Just ask Leung Wing-chuen, a long-time worker at salted fish distributor Hop Lee Ho in Sheung Wan.

"Salted fish is no longer the cheap food it once was," says Leung. "Some have the mistaken impression that salted fish are made from poor-quality fish. All the salted fish on this street come from us, because we're the manufacturer."

Hop Lee Ho might be a Hong Kong brand, but its operations are actually overseas. "Our factory in Bangladesh was opened by the owner in the 1970s, because there are too few fish in Hong Kong waters," Leung explains. "Hong Kong's salted fish [trade] is pretty much extinct."

The best way to prepare salted fish is to steam it, according to Leung. "You usually only eat a small portion at a time, since it's quite salty. If you want something with a lighter taste, head to the wet market and get yourself some fresh fish instead."

Leung wing-chuen, worker at Hop Lee Ho (合利號 *hup6 lay6 ho6*)

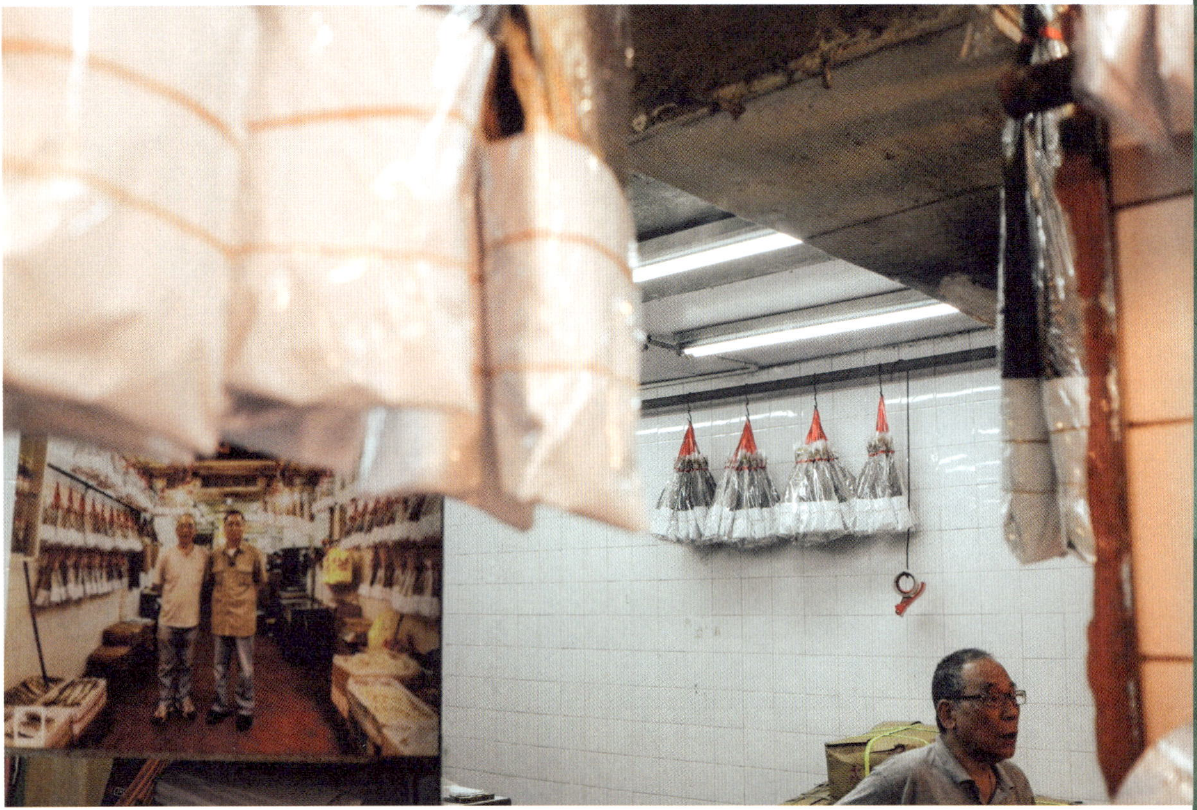

梅香馬友
每条
30完
遺失聲明
遺失啟事
美聯私家偵探社
香港私家偵探社
西貢
裝修

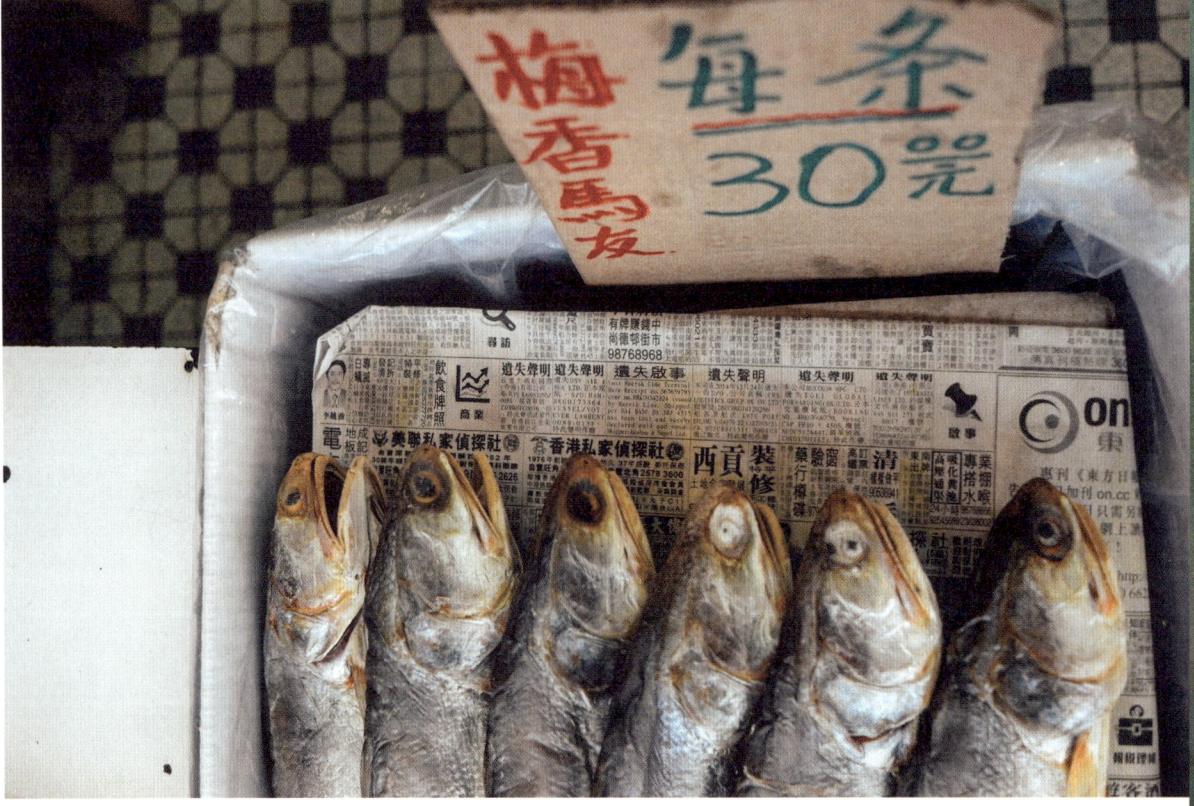

"Some have the mistaken impression that salted fish are made from poor-quality fish."

CHINESE-STYLE BRAISED DONKO SHIITAKE MUSHROOMS

燜冬菇伴菜心
mun1 dohng1 goo1 boon6 choy3 sum1

🕐 1 hr   🌙 1 night   👥 4-5 persons

A traditional dish, Chinese-style braised donko shiitake mushrooms are often eaten during family celebration dinners and added to traditional stews. This recipe produces soft, tender and flavorful mushrooms, perfect for eating with Cantonese noodles or paired with blanched vegetables.

INGREDIENTS

3 cloves garlic 蒜瓣 *sune3 fahn2*
2 slices ginger 薑片 *gurng1 peen2*
2 dozens dried donko shiitake
乾冬菇 *gawn1 dohng1 goo1*
1 catty (600g) choy sum 菜心 *choy3 sum1*
Salt, pepper 鹽, 胡椒 *yeem4, woo4 jiu1*

Peanut oil 花生油 *fah1 sung1 yau4*
Oyster sauce 蠔油 *ho4 yau4*
Rock sugar 冰糖 *bing1 tawng4*
Sesame oil 芝麻油 *jee1 mah4 yau4*
1 tablespoon cornstarch
生粉 *sahng1 fun2*

METHOD

Mushrooms

1. Cover dried mushrooms with tap water in a container, and soak overnight for at least 8 hours. Place heavy plate on top of mushrooms to submerge the pieces.

2. Chop ginger into slices and peel garlic cloves. With flat side of Chinese cleaver, smash ginger slices and garlic cloves to help release its flavors.

3. Heat peanut oil in large pot over medium-high heat. Add ginger and garlic. Cook until golden brown. Add mushrooms and soaking liquid into pot. Cook over high heat, about 15 minutes.

4. Add water into mix to ensure all mushrooms are submerged. Reduce heat to medium and cook for 30 to 45 minutes, until liquid reduces by more than half, and mushrooms are no longer submerged.

5. Mix one tablespoon of cornstarch with water. Add mixture into pot until liquid thickens to a sauce-like consistency.

6. Taste sauce, and season with salt, oyster sauce, rock sugar and sesame oil.

Choy Sum

1. Prepare slice of ginger and smash with flat side of Chinese cleaver. Meanwhile, bring pot of water to boil.

2. Heat peanut oil in wok or skillet over high heat. Add ginger and cook until fragrant. Add boiling water to wok. When it bubbles, season with pinch of salt. Add choy sum into water, and make sure water submerges the ingredients. Turn off fire immediately.

3. Blanch choy sum in water for 2 to 3 minutes, until center of stems appear translucent. Drain choy sum and serve.

FOOD FOR EVERY OCCASION

Food is a big part of most festivities in Hong Kong. Whether it's a religious ritual or an age-old tradition, almost everything can be celebrated, mourned, or symbolized with food. Here are just a few examples of the ways Hongkongers mark a special occasion with something edible.

SPECIAL OCCASIONS

CHINESE NEW YEAR
新年 *sun1 neen4*

Chinese New Year is one of the most festive occasions in Hong Kong. It's when businesses close for weeks at a time, and families get together for multi-course meals. Married couples and bosses give out lai see (利是 *lai6 see6*) red packets filled with crisp, unfolded bills. Flower markets pop up, lion dances abound, and there's usually a spectacular fireworks display by Victoria Harbour every year. Everything is decorated in lucky red and gold.

Of all the foods consumed during Chinese New Year, turnip cake (蘿蔔糕 *law4 bahk6 go1*) is right up there. Turnip cake is actually made from daikon or Chinese white radish rather than western-style turnip, and consists of a white mushy bundle of mashed radish strips with bits of dried shrimp or Chinese preserved sausage mixed in.

It's customary for families to serve this southern Chinese specialty to relatives visiting their homes. The cakes — which actually resemble puddings in texture — can be homemade or store bought, and are cut up into slices, then steamed or pan-fried.

The New Year pudding (年糕 *neen4 go1*) (literally, "year pudding") is another popular item that's served in the home. A sticky, gooey mound made from glutinous rice flour, the pudding is usually sliced into thin pieces and pan-fried before serving. The Chinese character for "pudding" sounds the same as the character for "tall" (高 *go1*), so New Year pudding is consumed in hopes of making one taller each year.

Some New Year dishes will be made with fat choy (髮菜 *faht3 choy3*) a moss-like bacteria that looks a lot like black human hair. Again, it's the auspicious-sounding name of fat choy that makes it a popular New Year food. The character for "fat" in Cantonese means "hair", but it also sounds identical to the character for "wealth" (發 *faht3*).

There are a whole bunch of other New Year-associated edible items and snacks, from sugar-coated winter melon (糖冬瓜 *tawng4 dohng1 gwah1*) and lotus seeds (糖蓮子 *tawng4 leen4 jee2*), to winter melon seeds (瓜子 *gwah1 jee2*). Meanwhile, the golden-orange kumquat fruit (金桔 *gum1 gutt1*) ("golden mandarin") is a visual representation of the color of wealth, and kumquat plants are especially prominent during the New Year.

WEDDINGS
婚禮 *fun1 lai5*

There is a whole set of rites and rituals for every traditional Cantonese wedding. A full Chinese banquet of multi-coursed, auspicious-sounding dishes is one. Pastry-giving is another.

There is one particular pastry — the "marrying daughter" cake (嫁女餅 *gah3 nui2 beng2*) — that is given by the bridegroom to the bride's family as part of the dowry ritual (過大禮 *gwaw3 dye6 lai5*) (literally, "passing of large gifts"). The "cakes", which take the form of sponge cakes, walnut cookies, or century egg and lotus seed paste variations are typically stamped with a "double happiness" (雙喜 *surng1 hay2*) or similarly happy-looking symbol on top. Modern tradition has the marrying couple handing out local bakery gift cards (餅卡 *beng2 kaht1*) to wedding guests instead of the actual pastry.

Tangyuan glutinous rice balls (湯圓 *tawng1 yune2*) filled with lotus seed paste are also served as desserts at wedding banquets. More on this in the following pages.

DRAGON BOAT FESTIVAL
端午節 *dune1 mm5 jeet3*

Dragon Boat Festival falls on the fifth day of the fifth month of the Chinese lunar calendar, and there are multiple theories on the origin of this holiday — from commemorating the death of a righteous poet to the worshipping of dragons. Today, Dragon Boat Festival has two hallmark components: dragon boat races and zongzi (粽 *johng2*) eating.

Zongzi are glutinous rice packets wrapped in bamboo leaves (or something similarly flat and wide), and they come in savory and sweet flavors. Savory zongzi can contain ingredients like pork, salted duck eggs and mung beans. Sweet zongzi are sometimes processed with Cantonese lye water to give them a distinct yellow hue, and might or might not contain any filling. According to legend, zongzi were thrown into the Miluo river to keep predatorial fish from eating the corpse of poet Qu Yuan, who committed suicide by jumping into its waters in 278 BCE.

BIRTH GIVING
產子 *chahn2 jee2*

Birth giving is a momentous occasion in any culture, but in Hong Kong, you also get a whole set of foods and rituals to go along with it.

For instance, after a woman gives birth, someone in the family — typically the woman's mother or mother-in-law — will cook up a stew of pork knuckles and whole eggs in a dark, sweet vinegar broth (豬腳薑醋 *ju1 gurk3 gurng1 cho3*) and serve the dish to visiting friends and family. The stew itself is said to be a nourishing treat for the baby's mother, and its main flavor comes from a viscous dark sweetened vinegar (甜醋 *teem4 cho3*) made from rice vinegar, spices and glutinous rice.

When the baby reaches its first month — dubbed "full moon" (滿月 *moon5 yute6*) in Chinese — there is usually a feast held in its honor. Eggs dyed in red or wrapped in lucky red paper (紅雞蛋 *hohng4 gai1 dahn2*) are given out to the guests: the eggs symbolize new life, and the color red stands for good fortune.

BIRTHDAYS
壽辰 *sau6 sun4*

Birthdays held at Chinese restaurants usually come with a staple of celebratory dishes. There's the longevity peach bun (壽包 *sau6 bao1*) — consisting of steamed, peach-shaped mantou buns filled with a sticky lotus seed paste and given a blush of pink on top — that's eaten as a dessert. Peaches are a common symbol of immortality in Chinese mythology, and so the peach buns are an especially suitable offering to someone who has reached another yearly milestone.

Another dish that's served on birthdays is yi mein noodles (see Rice and Noodles chapter), which are given the title longevity noodles (長壽麵 *churng4 sau6 meen6*) on the special occasion and served with the longevity peaches for an especially festive banquet.

MID-AUTUMN FESTIVAL
中秋節 *johng1 chau1 jeet3*

Mid-Autumn Festival, which occurs on the 15th day of the eighth month of the Chinese lunar calendar, is in essence a celebration of the full moon (and a mythical moon-dwelling goddess named Chang'e). On the night of the festival, the streets come alive with lit paper (and these days, plastic) lanterns, held by children walking through the neighborhood parks with their families.

It is also during this time that mooncakes (月餅 *yute6 beng2*) are consumed. There's a whole legend around these pastries: it is said that during the Yuan dynasty, when China was under Mongolian rule, the Han Chinese slipped secret messages into pastries to spread the word about a secret revolt. These pastries form the official origin story for modern-day mooncakes.

Traditionally, Cantonese-style mooncakes consist of a thin brown crust made from flour, peanut oil, Cantonese lye water and sugar syrup, and a dense filling of lotus seed paste and salted duck egg yolk. Each mooncake would have to be cut into pieces and shared, because it would be too heavy for one person to finish on their own.

However, Hongkongers have gotten creative over the years with their interpretation of the mooncake, and nowadays you can find them in all shapes and sizes, filled with any and every ingredient you can imagine. Creamy egg yolk custard has turned out to be one of the most popular fillings in recent years and nearly every five-star hotel will offer its own version every year.

FUNERALS
喪葬 *sawng1 jawng3*

Funerals in Hong Kong follow superstitions and traditions, descended from Taoist and Buddhist beliefs, that extend into food. For instance, a funeral meal (解穢酒 *gye2 wai3 jau2*) is typically hosted for guests after the ceremony, and during the meal, exactly seven dishes need to be ordered. There are multiple interpretations over the symbolism of the number seven in general — it is associated with both the concepts of life and death, depending on whom you ask. The memorial ritual itself can last between seven to 49 days (or seven weeks), allegedly stemming from a belief that the deceased goes through various stages of purgatory and redemption during that period.

The rites and superstitions extend to the white packets (吉儀 *gutt1 yee4*) that are given out at the funeral to guests, typically containing some candy, a dollar coin and a tissue. The candy signifies something "sweet" for the guests to take solace in after a day of sorrow, the tissue is for drying up tears, and the dollar coin is a small-gesture refund of any funeral contributions given by the guest, which the guest must use or spend before returning home, to avoid bad luck.

SPECIAL FOODS

POON CHOI
盆菜 *poon4 choy3*

Said to originate from the walled villages of the New Territories, poon choi is a celebration dish that is meant for sharing. The term poon choi literally means "basin food", and true to its definition, the dish is typically served in a large basin (today, metal basins are the most common). The ingredients of poon choi can vary, but dried donko shiitake mushrooms, poultry, pork, pork skin, daikon radish, fishballs and prawns are common elements. The ingredients are neatly stacked, layer by layer, right on top of each other in a circular pattern. The ingredients are cooked in a strong fermented soy-based sauce that gives the entire dish a predominant flavor.

Many guidelines exist for preparing poon choi, from the type of fire used to cook it (villagers historically preferred firewood) to the way the ingredients are stacked (daikon radishes, pork skin and other absorbent ingredients towards the bottom, more luxurious ingredients like seafood near the top). Poon choi is served on special occasions like weddings, Chinese New Year and Taoist festival Tai Ping Ching Chiu (太平清醮 *tye3 ping4 ching1 jiu3*) — where a vegetarian version is featured rather than the usual meat-laden affair.

In recent years, poon choi has been made more accessible to non-villagers via more and more restaurants offering the dish. It is also a popular dish to have during the colder winter months.

CHINESE BUDDHIST VEGETARIAN
齋 *jye1*

There's a particular type of vegetarian cuisine, known as Su vegetarian (素食 *so3 sick6*), that's affiliated with the Buddhists of the city. However, one should note that not all Buddhists are vegetarian, or practice vegetarianism permanently. The term "Su" also gets confusing because in Cantonese nowadays, it's taken to mean general vegetarianism, although it technically refers to vegetarians who avoid the Forbidden Five (五葷 *mm5 fun1*) "pungent" allium vegetables like garlic, scallion and coriander, as well as any animal product (the number five is not to be taken literally).

You'll find temples and Buddhist vegetarian restaurants offering the Hong Kong-ified version of Su vegetarian cuisine. Buddhist vegetarian cuisine differs from region to region, depending on local influences.

Some of the dishes can be quite distinct, and there is a category of meat-substitute dishes made predominantly from wheat gluten (麵筋 *meen6 gun1*). These meat substitutes are known collectively as zhai (齋 *jye1*) — but take note that the term zhai is also used to describe Buddhist vegetarian cuisine in general. You'd be surprised how close to the real deal these meat substitutes can be. They are even presented as chopped-up pieces of meat, marinated in colors reminiscent of their meat counterparts, and given textures that resemble skin and flesh.

TANGYUAN
汤圆 *tawng1 yune2*

Tangyuan, or glutinous rice balls, are traditionally a festival food item, although nowadays they can be eaten on any occasion and are a popular dessert at restaurants. Made from glutinous rice flour, the dumplings are bite-sized, round and sticky, and can contain different fillings like lotus seed paste, red bean paste or sesame paste. Glutinous rice dumplings are usually served in a sweet ginger- and brown or cane sugar-based soup.

The Chinese character for "yuan" (圆 *yune4*) sounds similar to the phrase for "union" (团圆 *tune4 yune4*), and so the dumplings are especially popular for family reunions. They are also eaten during weddings, winter solstice, and other festive occasions that see families getting together.

THE VILLAGE VOICE

South Garden Poon Choi Specialist is a restaurant that offers poon choi from the village of Pat Heung in Yuen Long, and Derrick Lai is its third-generation owner.

"We have been making poon choi since my grandfather's generation. Many of my ancestors are poon choi sifu in our village," Lai says. "The poon choi will consist of a slightly different mix of ingredients depending on the village or the chef."

As to how poon choi came to be, Lai believes that "the history can be traced back to when a Chinese emperor visited a walled village, and the villagers cooked a pot full of food for the emperor. Today, many villagers know how to make poon choi. It is common knowledge that has been passed down through the generations."

The essence of poon choi remains the same, but popular ingredients have changed over the years. "The ingredients have been updated slightly, compared to what I had growing up," Lai explains. "I remember having eel in my poon choi as a kid, but not so anymore. Probably because eel is trickier to prepare and cook."

"Today, many villagers know how to make poon choi."

Derrick Lai, owner of South Garden Poon Choi Specialist (南苑海鮮酒家 *nahm4 yune2 hoy2 seen1 jau2 gah1*)

KETCHUP PRAWNS

茄汁蝦
keh2 jup1 hah1

🕐 20 min   🍴 10 min   👥 4 persons

• •

Ketchup prawns is a very popular home-cooked dish for Chinese New Year. The word for "prawn" (蝦 *hah1*) sounds like the universal syllable for laughter — which is never a bad thing. The auspicious color of the ketchup-laced prawns also doesn't hurt!

INGREDIENTS

10 fresh prawns   蝦 *hah1*
1 spoon ketchup   茄汁 *keh2 jup1*
Worcestershire sauce   喼汁 *geep1 jup1*
Ginger   薑 *gurng1*
2 cloves garlic   蒜頭 *sune3 tau4*
Peanut oil   花生油 *fah1 sung1 yau4*

METHOD

1. Dice ginger and garlic and mix with ketchup and worcestershire sauce.

2. Heat wok over medium heat and add peanut oil. Put prawns into wok and fry until pink or about 70 percent cooked. Take out the prawns for later use.

3. Add sauce into wok, and fry for a few minutes until the sauce thickens. Turn fire to high heat, and add prawns into wok. Stir-fry prawns with sauce, until sauce thickens and sticks to prawns. Serve hot.

DINING ETIQUETTE

Every culture has its own implicit or explicit code of conduct to determine what's socially acceptable and what's not. Cantonese dining etiquette, in particular, is an enlightening glimpse into the city's collective values and expectations.

Of course, societal mandates have evolved over the years, but there will always be common themes. We have to thank seasoned food and travel writer Chan Chun-wai, a Hong Kong native who grew up in a strict household that takes table manners quite seriously, for a lot of the finer points in this chapter.

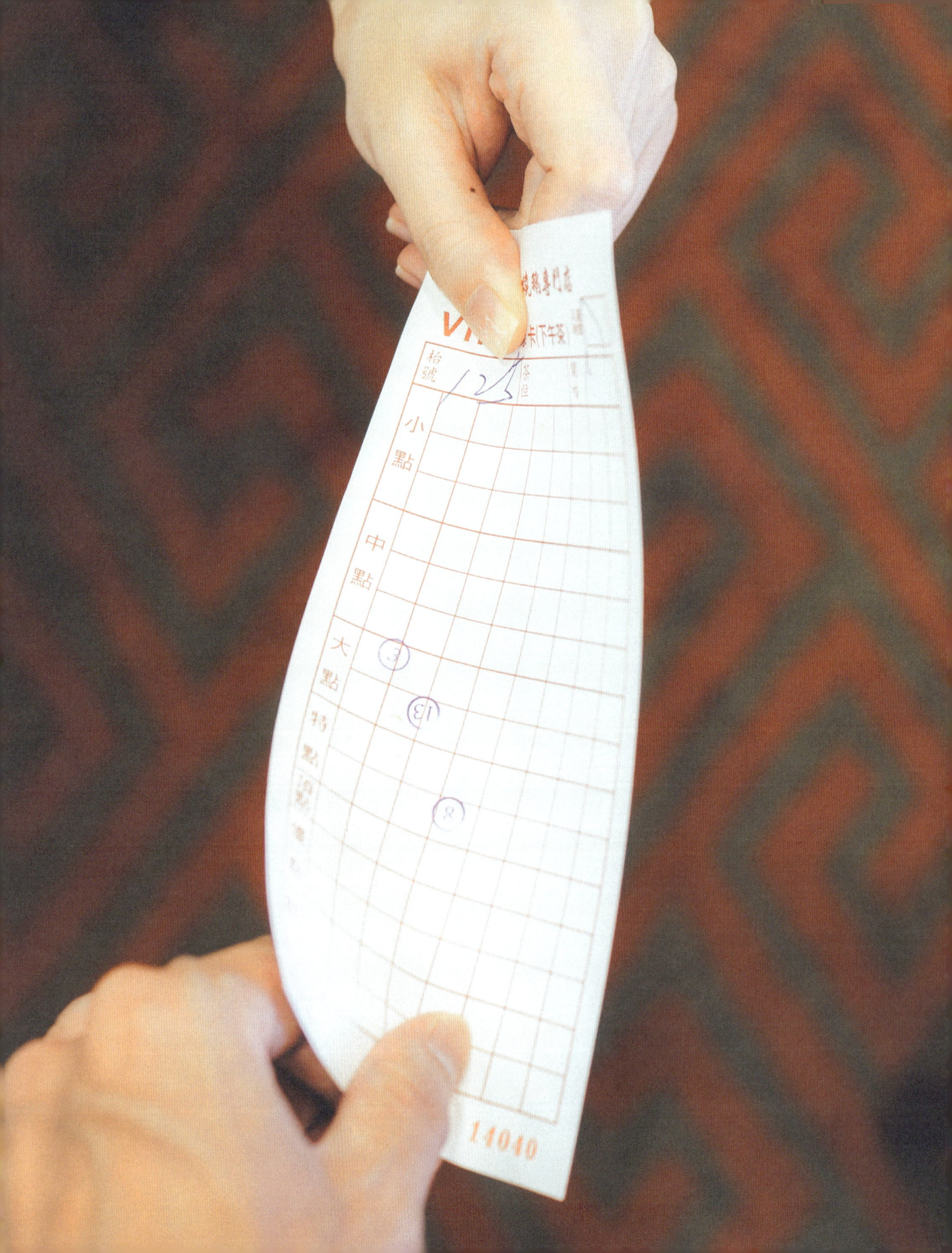

THE OLDER, THE WISER

Respect for elders is a prevalent motif in Cantonese culture, and this extends to how one behaves during meals with family, relatives and friends. From getting the best seats at the table to dictating who will eat the last piece of dumpling, the most senior members of a gathering usually have the most say. They will also take charge of ordering for the entire table, decide which tea will be served, and offer the final word on any decisions that need to be made.

KNOWING YOUR ROLE

There are different roles to be played at any given meal, and it's in everyone's best interest for the actors to know their parts. For instance, if you're having dinner with relatives or friends you haven't seen in a while, expect there to be a tug-of-war when the bill comes. The Chinese don't really believe in splitting the check, and it is a matter of courtesy for the host to pay for the table — even if it's sometimes difficult to figure out who the host might be.

But no matter who ends up footing the bill, there needs to be counterparties to put up a good fight. It can be interpreted as an insult for the host to settle the costs, uncontested — for who are these guests to take that generosity for granted? Therefore, it is crucial for all parties involved to understand the nuances of the situation, and to fulfill their duties regardless of the anticipated outcome.

DO THIS

- Let your elders have the best seats at the table. At a restaurant round table, this could mean the seats that are furthest away from the designated serving section (or the spot where the waitstaff will station themselves to serve the food for the whole table). It could also mean the seats closest to the bathroom, for extra convenience. The bottom line is, the elders should get to take their first pick of seats.

- Use your index and middle finger to tap lightly on the table whenever someone pours you tea. Legend has it that in the Qing dynasty, emperor Qianlong had once disguised himself as a commoner in a tea house, and when he went on to pour tea for his subject, the subject used his hands to demonstrate a kowtow (full bow) to thank his king without giving away their identities.

- Pour tea for the younger guests at the table, or for anyone you want to show respect to. The people doing the pouring also implicitly identify themselves as the hosts — and decision makers — of the table.

- At dim sum, wait for the tea to be served to the table before ordering food. The process is roughly translated as: "open with tea" (開茶 *hoy1 chah4*), and it highlights the significance of the beverage and how intricately it is linked with the food it is paired with.

- Help distribute food from the communal dishes to the younger members of the table and to anyone else within your reach. This shows your care and respect for those around you, and also implicitly positions you as a leader of the table.

- Use communal chopsticks when they are available, to pick from the communal dishes without leaving an imprint (like saliva from your personal chopsticks).

- Make sure the teapot lid is open when you need a refill at the table. Legend has it that sometime in the distant past, a diner had put his pet bird in the teapot at his table, and an unsuspecting server poured boiling hot water straight into the pot, killing the poor creature. It is now customary to lift the teapot lid and place it askew over the pot to indicate that a refill is needed.

- Lift your bowl off the table while eating. It's much easier to get rice from your rice bowl into your mouth this way — and there is even a term for it: to "shovel rice" (爬飯 *pah4 fahn6*). It also gives you better posture than if you were to hunch over the table.

- Feel free to leave bones on your plate. It might be unsightly, but when things start piling up, a smart server should be able to notice and swap a new plate for you.

DON'T DO THIS

- Don't poke your chopsticks into any food item if you can help it, as it is considered rude — and especially so when the item in question is a bowl of rice. Chopsticks inserted vertically into a mound of rice is reminiscent of a burning incense stick used for ancestor and deceased family member worship, and has no place at the dinner table.

- Don't try to eat anything with your hands: a spoon is used for liquids, and chopsticks are used for everything else. This includes items like chicken wings, whole prawns and fish with bones intact.

- Don't spill any rice on the table or leave any in your rice bowl. Rice was traditionally considered a precious commodity, and leaving any kernels uneaten is a sign of inconsiderate wastage.

- Don't leave any food item uneaten which someone else had served you, as it is considered rude. The best way to prevent this situation is to politely put your hand over your plate when someone tries to pass you a food item you don't want or cannot fully consume.

- Don't rotate the Lazy Susan at a roundtable before making sure that everyone has finished grabbing their food first.

- Don't take the last piece on any dish unless you're offering it to someone, or someone else is offering it to you.

COOKING TECHNIQUES

COOKING TECHNIQUES

Part of what makes Hong Kong- or Cantonese-style cooking so interesting is the sheer variety of methods available to process any one ingredient. Here are some of the most popular techniques.

STEAMING
蒸 *jing1*

Steaming is one of the quickest, easiest and healthiest ways to cook up a dish. It's also a quintessential Cantonese method, applied to everything from meat to eggs to leafy greens to tofu to fish. When you steam something, you essentially place it on a heat-resistant surface and subject it to the moist vapors of a boiling water source from below. An item that has been steamed will retain or even gain moisture, while losing any sharp textures. Dumpling skins turn soft and transparent; vegetables shed their raw crunch for a sweeter, subtler profile.

There are many high-tech gadgets and specialized steamers available in the market, but the only things you really need are a large pan or pot to hold some water; a small container to hold the ingredients; and some sort of trivet to keep the container above the boiling water. A resourceful Hongkonger would fill up the wok with water, place a metal steaming rack (蒸架 *jing1 gah2*) right in the center, then plop a ceramic plate, round stainless steel tray (鐵碟 *teet3 deep6*) or a bamboo container (竹蒸籠 *jook1 jing1 lohng4*) filled with raw ingredients over the rack. A wok lid would be used to contain the steam.

CHINESE-STYLE BRAISING
燜 mun1

Chinese-style braising essentially involves covering the surface of a pan or a wok with a shallow water-based sauce or broth; dunking the ingredients into the sauce; and simmering the ingredients and the sauce together for a short amount of time. The pan or wok typically remains uncovered.

Sometimes, Chinese-style braising calls for extra steps. Ingredients like meats are usually first stir-fried or toss-fried in a wok or pan. Then, before everything is fully cooked, the ingredients are simmered in a light layer of sauce or broth inside a covered pot until the sauce turns thick and concentrated.

When soy sauce is involved, the treatment is called red braising (紅燒 *hohng4 siu1* / 紅燜 *hohng4 mun1*) because of the reddish color the ingredients take on once cooked. You can braise meats, seafood, mushrooms… pretty much anything you want.

BOILING
煲 *bo1*

This might sound like an elementary technique, but Hongkongers take boiling quite seriously, especially when it comes to soups and noodle broths. Boiling in this context means mixing a combination of ingredients and seasoning with large amounts of water, then cooking everything all together in a pot, for as short as half an hour or as long as days. Soups that require extended cooking times aim for a reduction (熬 *ao4*) effect through the evaporation of water that keeps flavors strong and intense.

DOUBLE-BOILING
燉 *dun6*

Double-boiling (sometimes called double-steaming) might sound like a tedious procedure, but you're not doing anything twice here. Rather, double-boiling involves putting ingredients in a closed container filled with water, then putting that container in a pot or other cooking vessel filled with water, and subjecting everything to a slow and prolonged steam session. The closed container ensures that the evaporated liquid stays trapped inside, and none of the essence of the ingredients escapes. Double-boiling is reserved for luxurious ingredients like edible bird's nest, and delicate soups. There are specific ceramic containers made just for double-boiling purposes (see Tableware chapter).

STIR-FRYING
炒 *chao2*

Stir-frying, or the chao technique, is one of those popular methods that have pretty much become mainstream in kitchens and cookbooks around the world. With stir-frying, the wok is dry-heated to a very high temperature before a small to moderate amount of oil is drizzled from the sides down to the center. The ingredients are then tossed into the wok, starting with the ones that need more time to cook, and a wok spatula is used to "stir" the ingredients in a non-stop circular or quick-toss motion until everything is ready for consumption. Standard protocol calls for gripping the wok at an angle: you should hold it firmly using one hand, clutching close to the handle. Traditional woks are made entirely of metal and the handles are not insulated, so layering a cold wet cloth in between the hand and the wok for protection would be highly recommended. The gripping hand should be close to the heat source, and the wok should be tilted upwards, above the hand. The other hand is used for stirring. Depending on the weight of the wok, stir-frying can be quite a labor-intensive process, although It's also a relatively quick method that requires no more than 15 minutes of cooking time.

Properly stir-fried foods all possess one magical characteristic: wok hei (鑊氣, *wawk6 hay3*), or "wok essence." What this roughly equates to is that distinct smoky, charcoal-y, caramelized flavor that gets imparted to the ingredients as a result of using a wok under very high heat (above 200 degrees Celsius in professional kitchens).

SCALDING
灼 *churk3*

Scalding is the perfect technique for lazy people. All you have to do is bring a pot of water to a boil, drop your ingredients in, swirl them around for a few seconds, and that's it: you're done. Scalding is a good technique to use on thin slices of meat that cook easily, and even crispy leafy greens that you want to keep in their crispy green condition.

TOSS-FRYING
爆炒 *bao3 chao2*

Toss-frying is used to cook a moderate amount of ingredients in a very short amount of time. Instead of stirring the ingredients against the wok, you "toss" the ingredients in the air by jerking the wok itself. Sauce is sometimes added to the mix, but due to the high heat involved, the liquids tend to evaporate quite quickly. Foods treated by toss-frying are crisp and full of wok hei.

ROASTING
燒 *siu1*

Roasting is a technique that's not specific to Chinese cuisine, but one that's used quite extensively at specialty Hong Kong-style restaurants for whole poultry like chicken, duck and goose, as well as whole pigs. Roasting is definitely not a common household activity, as it requires a significantly large-sized oven or baking vessel and quite extensive preparations compared to other cooking methods. Having said that, Hongkongers living in village houses or in the outskirts of the city might own a makeshift brick oven in their backyards or open-air kitchens. Roasting involves subjecting food items, typically whole animal carcasses, to a dry convection-type heat source in a closed environment. The heat source has traditionally been charcoal, but nowadays most roasting ovens run on gas or electricity. Roasted meat turns crispy on the outside and evenly cooked on the inside. Different glazes or treatments applied to the meat beforehand will yield different results.

PAN-FRYING
煎 *jeen1*

Pan-frying is used for browning the surface of ingredients like tofu, dumplings or fish paste, and is usually done on a flat-surfaced pan — or, in the case of restaurants and street vendors, griddles. The cooking surface is coated with oil, and the ingredients are placed on top of the surface. Some ingredients might require flipping, and some ingredients might actually be cooked using a different method prior to pan-frying.

DEEP-FRYING
炸 *jah3*

Deep-frying is a perfected art in Cantonese cuisine, and the best part about it is you don't need specialty equipment to make it happen: all you need is a wok and some oil. Because of the wok's cylindrical structure, it doesn't take a lot of oil to fill out the bottom, making it a very efficient instrument for the task. Cantonese deep-frying refers to foods that are both partially or fully submerged in oil. Meat and seafood are common deep-fry candidates and can be coated in a batter beforehand, but even noodles, Chinese pastries and vegetables can be given the deep-fry treatment.

COOKING TREATMENTS

Besides cooking techniques, there are also popular cooking treatments that Hongkongers use on a regular basis.

SLOW-MARINATING
滷 *lo5*

Slow-marinating is essentially slow-cooking ingredients in a soy-sauce-based bath. It is especially popular amongst Hong Kong's Chiu Chow ("Chaozhou" in Putonghua) population. This technique is so popular that you'll find restaurants dedicated entirely to slow-marinated goods (see Local Restaurant Types chapter). Eggs, poultry and tofu are common items getting this treatment.

CORNSTARCH THICKENING
勾芡 *au1 heen3*

Hongkongers love to use cornstarch, especially to thicken their sauces. In fact, this treatment is so popular that there is a term for it: cornstarch thickening. Usually, the cornstarch is added at the end, turning a watery sauce into a thick, gooey solution that looks more appealing and can hold its own on a plate.

TENDERIZING / VELVETING
鬆肉 *sohng1 yook6*

There are some Cantonese beef and chicken dishes that consist of incredibly tender slices of meat. The secret to this is in the tenderizing or velveting process beforehand. There are many ways to achieve this result, but one common method is to marinate the meat in a mixture of egg white, rice wine and cornstarch first. At restaurants, the marinated meat would then be quickly cooked in hot oil, while at home, a pot of boiling water usually does the trick.

STIR-FRIED BEEF WITH GARLIC SHOOTS

蒜心炒牛肉
sune3 sum1 chao2 au4 yook6

🕐 15 min   🔪 10 min   👥 4 persons

In Cantonese cooking, beef is mostly presented as meatballs or slices. Stir-fried beef slices with different types of leafy greens make for an easy and popular dish in both restaurants and homes alike. You can also try tenderizing the beef if you prefer softer, chewier textures.

INGREDIENTS

4 taels (150g) beef 牛肉 *au4 yook6*
1 batch garlic shoots 蒜心 *sune3 sum1*
Onion 洋蔥 *yurng4 chohng1*
Ginger 薑 *gurng1*

Garlic 蒜頭 *sune3 tau4*
Chinese wine 酒 *jau2*
Peanut oil 花生油 *fah1 sung1 yau4*
Cornstarch 生粉 *sahng1 fun2*

METHOD

1. Cut garlic shoot into 2-inch pieces and slice onion. Dice garlic and cut ginger into slices. Cut beef into 2-inch-long slices. Heat the wok over high heat, add peanut oil and fry ginger and garlic until fragrant. Add in onion and stir-fry for about 2 minutes. Add garlic shoots and stir-fry until half cooked. Remove garlic shoot and onion from wok.

2. Add more peanut oil, and then toss in beef slices. Stir-fry beef until about 70 percent cooked, and put vegetables back into wok. Add one teaspoon water and Chinese wine, put the lid on, and let steam.

3. Meanwhile, mix cornstarch with water. Add mixture into wok to thicken sauce and intensify flavors. When sauce sticks to ingredients, serve.

BOILED CARROT AND CHINESE GREEN RADISH SOUP WITH PORK

青紅蘿蔔豬腱湯
cheng1 hohng4 law4 bahk6 ju1 jeen2 tawng1

🕐 2.5 hrs   🔪 10 min   👥 4 persons

Cantonese soups are a true delicacy. The essence of soup is derived from the meat or seafood that goes into its making. Fish and chicken are popular soup bases, and so is pork.

INGREDIENTS

1 catty (600g) pork leg muscle
豬腱 *ju1 jeen2*

1 carrot 紅蘿蔔 *hohng4 law4 bahk6*

1 Chinese green radish
青蘿蔔 *cheng1 law4 bahk6*

1 cob corn 粟米 *sook1 mai5*

1 piece dried tangerine peel
陳皮 *chun4 pay4*

Apricot kernels 南北杏 *nahm4 buck1 hung6*

Dried longan 龍眼乾 *lohng4 ahn5 gawn1*

Salt 鹽 *yeem4*

METHOD

1. Rinse vegetables, and cut carrot and Chinese green radish into medium pieces. Cut corn into 3 pieces but do not remove corn husk. Rinse pork and cut into pieces similar to the size of the vegetables.

2. Put all ingredients into pot and pour in unboiled water until it submerges all ingredients. Boil in high heat for about 30 minutes, skimming the white foam that forms on surface of water.

3. Turn fire down to low to medium heat and boil for about 2 hours. Add salt to your preference and serve.

DOUBLE-BOILED PAPAYA AND SNOW EAR FUNGUS SWEET SOUP

木瓜雪耳糖水
mook6 gwah1 sute3 yee5 tawng4 sui2

🕐 15 min   ⏲ 2-3 hrs   👥 4 persons

Despite this being called a soup, it really is a dessert and is meant to be served after a proper meal. The soft, squishy cooked papaya and gelatinous snow ear fungus provide an amazing textural contrast. This soup is light and delicate in flavor.

INGREDIENTS

1 piece snow ear fungus 雪耳 *sute3 yee5*

1 papaya 木瓜 *mook6 gwah1*

10-20 pieces apricot kernels 南北杏 *nahm4 buck1 hung6*

Rock sugar 冰糖 *bing1 tawng4*

METHOD

1. Soak apricot kernels and snow ear fungus in water 2 to 3 hours before cooking. Remove stem from snow ear fungus. Cut papaya and snow ear fungus into 1.5-inch pieces.

2. Put ingredients into a Chinese double-boiler, and fill with enough water to submerge ingredients. Put double-boiler into big pot shallowly filled with water. Boil for about 1.5 hours.

3. Before serving, add rock sugar to your preference.

TABLEWARE, UTENSILS AND COOKING EQUIPMENT

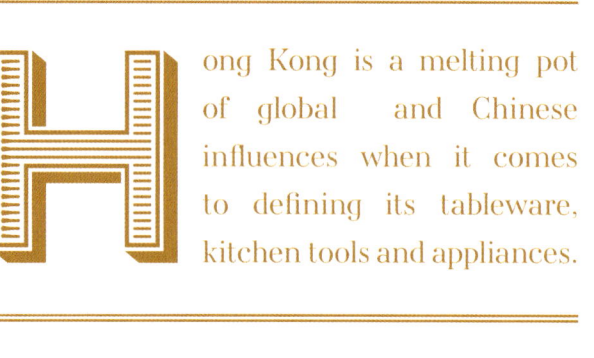

Hong Kong is a melting pot of global and Chinese influences when it comes to defining its tableware, kitchen tools and appliances.

COOKING EQUIPMENT

Although many general, non-culture-specific tools and gadgets can be found in a Hong Kong kitchen these days, Cantonese cooking does involve some specific equipment that one would not necessarily find in other styles of cooking.

WOK
鑊 *wawk6*

The all-purpose wok (鑊 *wawk6*) has become pretty mainstream these days, and hardly needs an introduction. The sphere-bottomed vessels are typically made from cast iron (生鐵 *sahng1 teet3*) or wrought iron (熟鐵 *sook6 teet3*), although you will also find stainless steel (不鏽鋼 *butt1 sau3 gawng3*), carbon steel (碳鋼 *tahn3 gawng3*) and aluminum (鋁 *lui5*) varieties. Wok diameters start from around 14 inches for home use, but can get much bigger for larger-scale cooking.

Hongkongers use the wok for absolutely everything: it is great for stir-frying, deep-frying, and even steaming. There are several handheld tools developed especially for the wok: the spatula (鑊鏟 *wawk6 chahn2*), the ladle (湯殼 *tawng1 hawk3*), the perforated scoop (炸篩 *jah3 sai1*) and the skimmer (笊籬 *sao1 lay1*). The spatula is used for stir-frying and to push objects around while deep-frying. The ladle, which is aligned nearly straight with the handle rather than perpendicularly or at an angle, is handy for spooning sauce and broth and can even be used in lieu of a spatula. The perforated scoop is great for picking up and separating chunky pieces of meat or greens that have been cooking in a thick sauce or broth. The skimmer is another essential tool in the kitchen: you can use it to pick up deep-fried items from the hot oil bath, and also to catch the strands of noodles that are cooking in broth. Extra-long wooden chopsticks (油炸筷子 *yau4 jah3 fye3 jee2*) are another handy item, used to pick up individual pieces from a wok. A bamboo wok brush (洗鑊掃 *sai2 wawk6 so2*) is all that's needed to clean the wok after each use. It's said that the bamboo bristles are gentler than conventional scrubs, removing the dirty bits without scraping off the seasoning that adds flavor to a veteran wok.

Many Hongkongers also use the wok for steaming. The wok is filled with a bit of water, and sometimes a steaming rack (蒸架 *jing1 gah2*) is placed at the bottom to prevent the steaming vessel from being submerged. If you're making dumplings, all you need is a simple bamboo steamer (蒸籠 *jing1 lohng4*) lined with parchment (蒸紙 *jing1 jee2*). If you're making steamed pork patty, steamed egg, or vegetables, you'll need to put the ingredients onto a metal plate (鐵碟 *teet3 deep2*) or ceramic plate instead. A wok lid (鑊蓋 *wawk6 goy3*) in this case would help contain the steam.

POTS
煲 *bo1*

Although not an essential household item, dedicated Hongkongers would boast a claypot (瓦煲 *ah5 bo1*) or two in their kitchen. The claypot is great for making rice dishes and casseroles, and conveniently doubles up as a serving dish.

There's also the Chinese double-boiler (燉鍋 *dun6 waw1*) (see our Cooking Techniques chapter), a ceramic container with two lids, typically used for cooking delicate soups and desserts. The pots come in single-portion to large-enough-to-feed-a-family sizes.

Traditional Chinese Medicine practitioners might have a Chinese herbs pot (中藥煲 *johng1 yurk6 bo1*) in their arsenal.

A shallow, wide-brimmed hot pot vessel (邊爐鍋 *been1 lo4 waw1*) — sometimes with a divider that splits the pot right down the middle — is another popular Hong Kong device for communal hot pot meals.

STOVES AND COOKERS

Every self-respecting Hongkonger would own a rice cooker (電飯煲 *deen6 fahn6 bo1*) at home. The rice cooker — essentially an electric heating device — is a one-step approach to preparing the staple commodity. You pour raw kernels into the rice container, submerge the kernels in water, then press a button and wait for the magic to happen. Within minutes, the kernels turn sticky and soft, becoming a pile of edible steamed rice.

For stovetop cooking, the open-flame gas stove (煤氣爐 *mooi4 hay3 lo4*) is the most popular option for Hongkongers, as it is a naturally good match for wok-cooking, which calls for intense, concentrated heat distributed over a non-flat surface. Locals can get their gas supplied by the city's utilities companies. For homes and businesses that are not connected to the city supply, there are companies offering refillable gas tanks that can be delivered straight to one's address.

For tabletop cooking in the form of hot pot meals — which is a favorite Hong Kong pastime — locals typically own a portable flat-surfaced electric stovetop (電爐 *deen6 lo4*) that can be easily stationed right on top of the dining table. Special mesh skimmers (火鍋笊籬 *faw2 waw1 sao1 lay1*) for each diner and a communal pot complete the setup.

KNIFE AND BOARD
刀, 砧板 *do1, jum1 bahn2*

The cleaver (菜刀 *choy3 do1*) is pretty much the only knife a Hongkonger needs in the kitchen. It's used for everything, from slicing and dicing, to chopping, flattening, pressing, and pounding. The round handle can even be used by the more skillful cooks to knead dumpling skins.

The perfect accomplice to the cleaver is the Chinese chopping board (砧板 *jum1 bahn2*), typically made of solid ironwood and cylindrical in shape; it looks like, and sometimes literally is, the cross-section of a tree trunk. This type of board is slightly higher maintenance (it's recommended to keep a damp cloth over the board when not in use, to prevent cracks from forming), but the surface is meant to be gentler on knife blades compared to plastic and other materials. Doesn't hurt that it also looks pretty handsome as a kitchen accessory!

ACCESSORIES

Cantonese cooking includes lots of boiling things in liquid, and one must-have item is the finely meshed soup bag (湯袋 *tawng1 doy2*), which conveniently keeps scraggly bits of food from infiltrating one's broth or medicinal soup.

Another handy accessory is the bamboo mat (竹墊 *jook1 jeen3*) that can be placed at the bottom of pots to prevent food from sticking to the pot's surface while cooking.

When it comes to uniquely Hong Kong table settings, toothpick holders (牙籤筒 *ah4 cheem1 tohng2*), mini soy sauce containers (豉油樽 *see6 yau4 juhn1*) and chili sauce jars (辣椒油樽 *laht6 jiu1 yau4 juhn1*) are a common theme at casual diners and restaurants as well as in homes.

TABLEWARE

A meal in Hong Kong is typically a communal affair. At the dinner table, the setup is such that dishes of meat and vegetables, collectively known as accompaniments (餸 *sohng3*), are laid out in the center for sharing, and a bowl filled with rice is given to everyone taking part in the meal. The sizes and shapes of the bowls and plates used, all reflect this sharing mentality.

RICE BOWL
飯碗 *fahn6 woon2*

The rice bowl is the principal vessel that's used for nearly every type of Hong Kong-style meal. It's used to hold soups before the meal starts, and to hold the rice during the meal. Lots of Cantonese desserts are in soup form, so a second bowl could make an appearance at the end of the meal. Rice bowls are designed so that they can be held in one hand, and it is acceptable to lift the bowl off the table when eating.

CHINESE SPOON
匙羹 *chee4 gung1*

There's the spoon, and then there's the Chinese spoon. Typically made from ceramic (although plastic varieties are also quite common), the Chinese spoon has a very distinguishable flat surface that enables it to balance perfectly on the table. The spoon is used almost exclusively for drinking soups and liquids. Although one might be tempted to also use it for scooping up rice and other bits from a bowl, proper etiquette calls for chopsticks to perform this duty.

CHINESE PLATES
中式碟 *johng1 sick1 deep2*

Plates come in all sorts of shapes and sizes in Hong Kong restaurants and homes. There are the large oval plates (大橢圓碟 *dye6 taw5 yune4 deep2*) that hold large whole steamed fish or meats to be consumed sharing-style around the dinner table. There are the small round communal sauce dishes (豉油碟 *see3 yau4 deep2*) to hold the condiments that accompany the main courses. At restaurants, each individual diner also typically gets a medium-sized circular plate (圓碟 *yune4 deep2*) to use as an all-purpose surface — for instance, to hold bones, or to handle excess food items that don't fit into the rice bowl.

CHINESE TEAWARE
中式茶具 *johng1 sick1 chah4 gui6*

In terms of Cantonese-style beverage vessels, the dainty Chinese teacup (中式茶杯 *johng1 sick1 chah4 booi1*) inevitably comes to mind. The small tapered cups are made from ceramic and can be held neatly in one hand. They are most often used in dim sum halls and Chinese restaurants. Fancier versions come with a matching lid and saucer. Tea is always served hot, filled close to the brim — from a Chinese teapot (中式茶煲 *johng1 sick1 chah4 bo1*) that is especially stout and shallow. Chinese tea connoisseurs might sometimes splurge on a set of highly prized unglazed Yixing clay teaware (紫砂壺 *jee2 shah1 woo2*) for their home collection. The clay's unglazed surface is said to absorb the flavors of the drink it is holding — which means the teas become more complex with each pour. Remember to use a separate pot for each type of tea to keep the flavors pure.

CHOPSTICKS 筷子 *fye3 jee2*

Chopsticks are an essential utensil for every Hongkonger. The most common variety is made from an off-white melamine material that vaguely resembles ivory. Actual ivory chopsticks were once an esteemed item — legend has it they change color when they come in touch with poison (convenient for the paranoid diner). However, in 1989 the ivory trade effectively became illegal when the African elephant was placed on an international endangered species list. These days, you'll still find antique and furniture shops in Hong Kong legally touting pre-1989, government-licensed ivory chopsticks.

Chinese chopsticks are square-shaped at the top, and circular at the bottom. This is in contrast to pointy wooden Japanese chopsticks, or flat metal Korean chopsticks. It's quite common to set up a table with a pair or more of communal chopsticks, laid close to the communal dishes and within easy reach of everyone. The communal chopsticks are sometimes a different color or length from the individual chopsticks, to prevent confusion. The communal chopsticks are shared by all diners, who use them to pass food from the different communal dishes back to their own bowls.

A FULL PLATE

Yuet Tung China Works has been manufacturing and exporting handmade porcelain tableware since 1928. One of Yuet Tung's specialties is Kwon-glazed porcelain (廣州彩瓷 *gwawng2 jau1 choy2 chee4*), a specific painting style that came out of Guangdong province several hundred years ago.

"Kwon-glazed porcelain was originally known as China Trade Porcelain (外銷瓷 *oy6 siu1 chee4*) — it was mostly made for foreign markets, so you hardly see them in local shops," Joseph Tso, third-generation owner, tells us. "Kwon-glazed porcelain goes back about 300 years." But Tso gives us a history lesson that goes further back. "The making of porcelain began in Jingdezhen (景德鎮 *ging2 duck1 jun3*), in Jiangxi province. The industry was originally confined within China. It wasn't until the Qing Dynasty that the Guangzhou ports opened to foreign traders," Tso explains.

"The porcelain manufactured in Jingdezhen was designed for domestic and commercial use," he continues. "Many of the foreign traders started requesting their own family crests or scenic paintings or patterns on them. So some clever local businessmen hired a few craftsmen from Jingdezhen, bought plain porcelain from Jingdezhen, and set up a factory in Guangzhou, training people from Guangzhou to paint porcelain."

The style of overglaze porcelain painting (釉上彩 *yau4 surng6 choy2*) that developed in Guangzhou eventually evolved into Kwon-glazed porcelain. "Kwon-glazed porcelain is known for its elaborate, splendid designs. Popular patterns include roses," Tso says.

"We no longer make Kwon-glazed porcelain at Yuet Tung the way it was made during my grandfather's time, because it requires more steps and skills," Tso says. "Very few Hong Kong companies still do traditional Kwon-glazed porcelain. We used to hire people from Peng Chau and Cheung Chau to paint the colors onto the porcelain. It took each person around two days to finish a porcelain piece — in today's market, you just can't afford that kind of cost."

> "Kwon-glazed porcelain is known for its elaborate, splendid designs. Popular patterns include roses."

Joseph Tso, owner of Yuet Tung China Works (粵東磁廠 *yute6 dohng1 chee4 chawng2*)

A DIFFERENT INTERPRETATION

Decades ago, Peng Chau was home to a bustling tableware industry, but these days only a few tableware shops remain. Chiu Kee is one of them: it's owned by Lam Kiu, who used to run the operation with her late husband.

"None of the tableware factories stayed in Peng Chau," Lam tells us. "This street used to be lined with factories. They have all closed down. All of them moved away — some to mainland China, some to Cheung Chau."

Back in the day, Chiu Kee specialized in Kwon-glazed porcelain, a specific painting style from Guangdong. Today, Lam bases her tableware designs on her own whims. "The patterns I create now on plates and bowls are very much different than those from the old days," she says.

Lam Kiu, owner of Chiu Kee (超記瓷器 *chiu1 gay3 chee4 hay3*)

"I have more freedom now to paint what I want, but in the past, we did it in a very traditional style, based on what the clients wanted. Now our products are treated more like art, but back then they were just bowls and plates with the regular patterns."

"There are theories on the meaning behind traditional patterns like goldfish and chicken," Lam continues. "But to me, they don't matter that much. I focus on what looks beautiful on the porcelain. My late husband especially liked to invent new patterns or new ways of drawing traditional patterns."

"Now our products are treated more like art, but back then they were just bowls and plates with the regular patterns."

REFERENCES

Not necessarily recommended or endorsed

BOOKS
By Author

Flaws, Bob. The Tao of Healthy Eating: Dietary Wisdom According to Traditional Chinese Medicine. Colorado: Blue Poppy, 1998. Print.

Lee, Jonathan H. X. Chinese Americans: The History and Culture of a People. San Francisco: ABC-CLIO, 2015. Print.

Liu, Junru. Chinese Food. Cambridge: Cambridge UP, 2011. Print

Mente, Boye De. Etiquette Guide to China: Know the Rules That Make the Difference. Tokyo: Tuttle Publishing, 2008. Print.

O. Hollmann, Thomas. The Land of the Five Flavors: A Cultural History of Chinese Cuisine. New York: Columbia UP, 2013. Print.

Shookman, Pam. The Chinese Wet Market Handbook. Hong Kong: Blacksmith Books, 2014. Print.

Tsang, Steve. A Modern History of Hong Kong. New York: IB Taurus & Co., 2004. Print.

方芳。精挑細選南北貨。萬里機構，飲食天地出版社，2013。書籍。

甘健成。鏞樓甘饌錄。香港：經濟日報出版社，2006。書籍。

陳夢因 [特級校對]。食經 壹 平常真味。香港：商務印書館，2007。書籍。

陳夢因 [特級校對]。食經 貳 不時不食。香港：商務印書館，2007。書籍。

陳夢因 [特級校對]。食經 叁 烹小鮮如治大國。香港：商務印書館，2007。書籍。

陳夢因 [特級校對]。食經 肆 南北風味。香港：商務印書館，2007。書籍。

陳夢因 [特級校對]。食經 伍 廚心獨運。香港：商務印書館，2007。書籍。

蔡瀾。蔡瀾食材字典。濟南：山東畫報出版社，2008。書籍。

蔡瀾。蔡瀾食材字典續編。濟南：山東畫報出版社，2008。書籍。

By Title

Barbecue: A Global History. Jonathan Deutsch and Megan J. Elias. University of Chicago Press, 2014. Print.

Chinese America: Histaory and Perspectives 1999. San Francisco: Chinese Historical Society of America, 1999. Print.

Rice Almanac: Source Book for the Most Important Economic Activity on Earth. J.L. Maclean, David Charles Dawe, and Gene P. Hettel. Oxon: CABI Publications, 2002. Print.

Your Guide to Health with Foods & Herbs: Using the Wisdom of Traditional Chinese Medicine. Yifang Zhang and Yingzhi Yao. New York: Better Link, 2012. Print.

粵式酒樓美食。香港：萬里機構，飲食天地出版社，2012。書籍。

傳統粵菜精華錄。陳夢因、江獻珠。香港：萬里機構，2005。書籍。

廚師及燒臘師手冊。陳照炎、趙丕揚、胡列夫。香港：萬里機構，2003。書籍。

WEBSITES & ONLINE ARTICLES

Changing Guangzhou's Name to Canton Will Raise City's International Profile, Delegate Suggests. South China Morning Post. 2014.

Guide to Import of Mainland Chilled Chickens into HK. Centre for Food Safety - Imported Food Control. 2015.

Hawker Control - Overview. Food and Environmental Hygiene Department. 2016.

Highly Valued Rice Fragrance Has Origins in Basmati Rice, Study Finds. Cornell Chronicle. 2009.

History of Fermented Black Soybeans (165 B.C. to 2011). Soyinfo Center. 2012.

History of Soybeans and Soyfoods in China and Taiwan. Soyinfo Center. 2012.

Hong Kong's 'legal' ivory trade thrives on folk beliefs and China's rising wealth. Independent. 2013.

Policy on inheritance of dai pai dong culture. Tommy Cheung, Legislative Council Member. 2005.

Report of Subcommittee on Hawker Policy. Panel on Food Safety and Environmental Hygiene, Legislative Council Paper No. CB(4)1497/14-15. 2015.

Review on Hawker Licensing Policy. Advisory Council on Food and Environmental Hygiene, Food and Health Bureau. 2009.

7 Things About Tea. Leisure and Cultural Services De*partment*. 2012.

食字號(1)：一盅兩件走入歷史. 蘋果日報. 2008.

食典：在水中央擦正宗避風塘炒蟹. 蘋果日報. 2011.

食肆改用煤氣熱風烤燒豬. 蘋果日報. 2004.

香港「街頭小食」與香港文化認同. Department of Cultural Studies, Lingnan University. 2007. Web.

廣州「一口通商」成食污黑點. 灼見名家. 2015.

精明消費：木憲木砧板質料硬淨夠生. 蘋果日報. 2005.

喀什百年茶館—道不盡絲路老城千年茶味. 新華網. 2015.

避風塘炒蟹少油快兜. 蘋果日報. 2006. Web.

鮮甜大白菜 同步過冬. 東方日報. 2014. Web.

cculture.hku.hk

www.chiculture.net

www.heritagemuseum.gov.hk

ricepedia.org

INTERVIEWEES

Blackie Hui | Chan Chun-bun, Hing Kee | Chan Chun-wai, travel and food writer | Chui Chin Kam-yi, Yick Cheong Ho | Chui Kwok-hing, Sun Hing Restaurant | CK Chan, Yu Hing | Derrick Lai, South Garden Poon Choi Specialist | Elaine Lam, Good Spring Company Chinese Herbal Pharmacy | Gary Chan, Har Kee Noodles | Gladys Leung, TCM Dr. Gladys Leung Clinic | Hardy Kam, Kam's Roast Goose | Mrs. Ho, Chuen Cheong Foods | Ken Wong, Kowloon Soy Company | Jason Lam, Lam Cheong Kee | Joseph Tso, Yuet Tung China Works | Kenneth Lee, Oi Man Sang | Lam Kiu, Chiu Kee | Lau Kin-wai, Kin's Kitchen | Mr. Lee, Kwan Kee Bamboo Noodles | Mr. Leung, Loy Kee Meat Stall, Shui Wo Street Market | Leung Kwan, Man Lee Leung | Leung Wing-chiu, Tung Hing Tai Kee | Leung Wing-chuen, Hop Lee Ho | Martin Lam, Good Spring Company Chinese Herbal Pharmacy | Nelson Law, Fat Kee Noodles | Mrs. Ng, Shui Wo Street Market | Patrick Yeung, Fukien Tea Company | Rose Cheuk, Station Tofu Pudding | Sherman Ho, Chuen Cheong Foods | Stephen Law, Gateway Cuisine | Sze Wing-ching, Lin Heung Kui | Tong Sung-chiu, Lemon King | Tsang Sau-yuen, Bak Cheung Tong | Wayne Wu, Oi Man Sang | Wong Kwan-seng, Kam's Roast Goose | Wong Tak-kam, Shing Hing Tai Rice Shop | Yannie Chan Sin-yan

PHOTOS

Chak Kee Noodles | Chiu Kee | Chuen Cheong Foods | Bak Cheung Tong | Fat Kee Noodles | Fat Kee Noodles | Fei Jie | Fukien Tea Company | Gateway Cuisine | Good Spring Company Chinese Herbal Pharmacy | Har Kee Noodles | Hing Kee | Gateway Cuisine | Hop Lee Ho | Hot Pot Instinct | Kam Fung Restaurant | Kam's Roast Goose | Kowloon Soy Company | Kwan Kee | Kwan Kee Bamboo Noodles | Lam Cheong Kee | Lemon King | Lin Heung Kui | Loy Kee Meat Stall | Man Lee Leung | Oi Man Sang | Queen Road's Central | Sai Yeung Choi Street South | Shau Kei Wan Main Street East | Shing Hing Tai Rice Shop | Shui Wo Street Market | Smithfield Market | South Garden Poon Choi Specialist | Star Seafood Restaurant | Station Tofu Pudding | Sun Hing Restaurant | Tai On Building | Tai Wing Wah Restaurant | TCM Dr. Gladys Leung Clinic | Tung Hing Tai Kee | Yick Cheung Ho | Yu Hing | Yuen Kee Dessert | Yuet Tung China Works